# THE PROBLEM OF
# IMMIGRATION

edited by STEVEN ANZOVIN

## THE REFERENCE SHELF

Volume 57 Number 1

*104427*

THE H. W. WILSON COMPANY

New York   1985

# THE REFERENCE SHELF

The books in this series contain reprints of articles, excerpts from books, and addresses on current issues and social trends in the United States and other countries. There are six separately bound numbers in each volume, all of which are generally published in the same calendar year. One number is a collection of recent speeches; each of the others is devoted to a single subject and gives background information and discussion from various points of view, concluding with a comprehensive bibliography. Books in the series may be purchased individually or on subscription.

**Library of Congress Cataloging in Publication Data**

Main entry under title:

The Problem of immigration.

(The Reference shelf ; v. 57, no. 1)
Bibliography: p.
1. United States—Emigration and immigration—Addresses, essays, lectures.   2. United States—Emigration and immigration—Government policy—Addresses, essays, lectures.   I. Anzovin, Steven.   II. Series.
JV6455.P76   1985          325.73          84-29941
ISBN 0-8242-0710-6

Printed in the United States of America

# THE
# REFERENCE
# SHELF

# CONTENTS

IV. POLICY AND REFORM

V. A WORLD PROBLEM

# PREFACE

Viewed dispassionately, immigration may seem to obey some physical law analogous to that governing the movement of gases. As a gas under pressure will rush to fill an empty connecting vessel, so population growth in poor areas tends to push masses of people toward more sparsely populated or wealthier areas until conditions are roughly equalized. But this simple model does not convey the more complex problems of human migration. Although for the immigrants themselves immigration is usually a blessing, for societies and nations it can be an economic and cultural disaster. The poor nations lose many of their most talented and valuable members to the richer nations, while the developed countries, often hampered by shortsighted policies that institutionalize a greed for cheap labor, worry about how to maintain their standards of living in the face of massive influxes of new, perhaps incompatible citizens. The wretched hordes of political and economic refugees, the seemingly ungovernable flow of illegal immigration, and the problems of racism and religious hatred only exacerbate the problem. Above all, the unprecedented growth of the world's population makes the task of developing a global code of conduct for immigration particularly urgent.

The United States, the richest nation on earth, is a magnet for many of the world's immigrants. And, by and large, America has been generous in accepting the "huddled masses" of other countries. That part of the national image is one most Americans, remembering their own roots as immigrants, are especially proud of. However, it is not clear whether the U.S. wants to continue in the role of "mother of exiles." In the past, high rates of immigration have caused xenophobia in those already here, expressed in restrictive, sometimes cruel immigration policies. The 1920s and 1950s were such periods, and the nation appears to be entering yet another. At issue is not only the cohesiveness of American society, but also its conception of itself as open and pluralistic. Can the United States afford to risk losing its wealth and national unity by welcoming the disparate masses who wish to enter, or will it close its borders, opting for safety and stagnancy?

5

This compilation of reprinted articles and essays presents the major aspects of the problem of immigration as they affect the policies and society of the United States. The articles in Section I describe the immigrants coming to the United States today and the anxiety felt by Americans over their effect on the country. Section II focuses on illegal immigration, presenting arguments for and against stopping the flow. Section III covers United States refugee policy and discusses its ethical aspects. The current heated debate over U.S. immigration policy reform is dealt with in Section IV. Finally, Section V touches upon the international nature of the problem. Its three articles discuss the need for an international agreement on immigration.

The editor wishes to thank the authors and publishers who have kindly granted permission to reprint the material in this collection. Special thanks are also due to the staffs of the Englewood (New Jersey) Public Library and the New York Public Library System, and to Diane Podell of the B. Davis Schwartz Memorial Library, C.W. Post Center, Long Island University.

Steven Anzovin

March 1985

# I. THE GOLDEN DOOR

## EDITOR'S INTRODUCTION

The immigrant experience is central to the national psyche. Most Americans are the descendants of immigrants who came to the United States in the last century and a half; many now living remember the struggles of their parents to succeed in the new land. Popular novels and films repeatedly work variations on the classic American saga of the penniless immigrant who makes his or her fortune through determination and luck. Politicians invoke their immigrant antecedents as proof of their capacity for hard work and self-sacrifice.

Between 600,000 and 800,000 legal immigrants will enter the United States this year. It is safe to assume that most regard their entry into the United States as a passage through a "golden door"—as Emma Lazarus called it in her poem "The New Colossus"—into a land of unlimited opportunity. And, to judge from articles in this section, life in America can be as promising for the new immigrants as the popular myths may lead them to believe. But how, in a nationalistic and conservative era, do Americans feel about the flood of newcomers?

James Fallows, writing in the *Atlantic*, introduces the character of immigration today—the numbers and kinds of immigrants, recent changes in immigration policy, and the scope of national concern. What are the immigrants doing to American society? Fallows asks. Robert Lindsey's report, reprinted from the *New York Times Magazine*, describes the rapid assimilation of Asian immigrants and the impact that their presence has had upon American culture and business. The assimilation of immigrants is seen from another perspective in an article from *Black Enterprise* by Udayan Gupta, who describes the resentment of those American minority groups who feel that the influx of immigrants deprives them of scarce opportunities to work.

## IMMIGRATION:
## HOW IT'S AFFECTING US[1]

It was "noble, revolutionary—and probably the most thought-less of the many acts of the Great Society." Thus did Theodore White, chronicler of all that is brave and optimistic about America, assess in 1982 the thing his country had done to itself seventeen years earlier. He was not talking about the decision to increase the commitment of American ground forces to South Vietnam, nor about the beginning of programs that would end in racial quotas and school-busing orders, nor about the inauguration of Medicare and other benefits whose costs the public would in the 1980s be struggling to pay. Rather, this most thoughtless gesture was the Immigration and Nationality Act amendments of 1965.

The new laws were not expected to increase the flow of immigrants to this country. Indeed, for the first time in America's history, they put limits on the numbers that could enter from Mexico, the Caribbean, and elsewhere in the Western Hemisphere. But the laws did revolutionize the nature of the immigrant population. Back in the 1920s, when the U.S. first placed limits on the number of immigrants it would accept, the central principle of immigration policy was that America's new citizens should resemble its old ones. Under the "national-origins" system introduced in 1921, quotas for European immigration preserved the "racial preponderance" within the American population. Ireland, for example, could send each year 3 percent as many immigrants as there were foreign-born Irish-Americans counted in the U.S. Census of 1910. (In 1924, the quotas were made more restrictive. They were set at 2 percent of the ethnic representation among Americans, foreign-born and native-born, shown in the 1890 Census.) The national-origins system was designed as a shield against the "New Immigration" of Poles, Italians, Slavs, and Eastern European Jews.

[1]Excerpted from a magazine article by James Fallows, Washington editor of the *Atlantic*. *Atlantic*. 252:45+. N. '83. Copyright © 1983 by James Fallows. Reprinted by permission.

With the Immigration Act amendments of 1965, the United States announced that it would look impartially on the world. The Ethiopian, the Turk, the resident of Calcutta or Rangoon, would compete on equal footing with the Englishman and the German. America would open itself not merely to the tired and the poor but to the racial and ethnic balance of the wide world. The result, wrote Theodore White, was "a stampede, almost an invasion." The "sources of fresh arrivals [would be] determined not by those already here, but by the push and pressures of those everywhere who hungered to enter."

Those pressures are sobering to contemplate. According to the International Labour Organization, the total labor force of the Third World countries will be 600 million to 700 million people larger in the year 2000 than it was in 1980. To employ all those additional workers, the developing countries would have to create more jobs than now exist in Western Europe, Japan, the United States, the Soviet Union, and the other industrialized nations combined. Obviously, that will not happen, and some of those who cannot find work, especially in Latin America, will decide to leave.

"Especially" Latin America because the riches of the United States lie within easy reach of so much of Central and South America, and because population growth there is exceptionally fast. The combined population of the Latin American nations was about 150 million in the early 1950s. It is expected to be 845 million by 2025. Half of the people in Latin America are eighteen years old or under; they will be entering the labor force, looking for work in their countries or ours, in the next generation. Robert Fox, of the Inter-American Development Bank, points out that the total Latin American labor force is now about 115 million, but will be 197 million twenty years from now. "This is intractable," he has said. "It is based on a population already born. Latin American countries would have to create an average of 4 million new jobs each year until 2025 [to accommodate the growth]. The U.S., with an economy five times larger, averages 2 million new jobs per year."

Regardless of these projections, the flow of immigrants from the Third World has already begun. From 1930 to 1960 about 80 percent of America's immigrants came from European countries or Canada. From 1977 to 1979, 16 percent did, and Asia and Latin America accounted for about 40 percent each. In 1979, the nine leading "source" countries for legal immigration were Mexico, the Philippines, Korea, China and Taiwan, Vietnam, India, Jamaica, the Dominican Republic, and Cuba. In tenth place, with 3 percent of the total, was the United Kingdom.

The structure of the immigration code meant that the Third World's share of new Americans was likely to increase. Under the post-1965 law, places in the immigration queue are assigned with grand indifference to ethnic origin but with careful attention to family ties. The immediate relatives of American citizens— parents, minor children, and spouses—are admitted without limit. In recent years, some 150,000 people have entered this way annually. In addition, the law provides for 270,000 immigrants each year (no more than 20,000 from any one country) in the "numerically limited" categories, which heavily favor less-immediate relatives. Eighty percent of the 270,000 places are allotted to the adult children or the brothers and sisters of U.S. citizens, plus the immediate relatives of non-citizens who are here as permanent resident aliens. The remaining places go to those with skills considered valuable to the American economy, or to those who would simply like to come. The law's premium on family connections means that each new arrival from the Philippines or Korea eventually makes many others in those countries eligible for admission.

Beyond this change in the mix, there has been a change in numbers. In 1980, at least 125,000 Cubans and Haitians arrived in southern Florida and were admitted as "special entrants," a category invented to cope with the influx. Since 1975, the U.S. has accepted over half a million refugees from Indochina. More than 160,000 came in 1980 alone, which together with the Cubans and Haitians pushed that year's total for legal admissions to 808,000, the highest in sixty years.

And this is to speak only of lawful entrants. As Latin America's population has grown and its governments and economies have foundered, more and more of its people have looked northward for relief. In the mid–1970s, the commissioner of the Immigration and Naturalization Service, Leonard Chapman, said that there might be as many as 12 million foreigners here illegally. Official estimates are now 50 to 75 percent lower than that, but no one can say with confidence how many illegal aliens are here and how many more are coming. In many of the big cities of the north, throughout the southwestern states, and in the labor-intensive farming regions of the east and west coasts, daily life provides signs of the illegal tide. Early this year, the attorney general of the United States, William French Smith, proclaimed, "Simply put, we've lost control of our own borders."

As the immigrants continue to arrive, the alarm bells have begun to ring. From liberals and conservatives alike have come warnings about the implications of the trend. Clare Booth Luce, the venerable Republican, has said that the immigrants will be more difficult to absorb because they are not white. Carl Rowan, a black Democrat, has written about the "immigration nightmare." Ray Marshall, secretary of labor in the Carter Administration, has claimed that we could worry much less about unemployment if we got rid of illegal immigrants. Jesse Helms and Paula Hawkins, two of the most conservative members of the U.S. Senate, have argued that if the U.S. doesn't help defeat the guerrillas in El Salvador, we will be flooded with Salvadoran refugees, as we were with refugees from Vietnam. Labor leaders have issued statements saying that immigrant workers are stealing Americans' jobs.

"Our immigration policy is making us poorer, not richer," Richard Lamm, the Democratic governor of Colorado, said this year. "It is dividing our wealth and resources." Last year, Lamm contended that America's economic "pie" had stopped growing and that "the unchanging pie dramatically alters an issue like immigration, for now additional people will have to take from that pie rather than contribute to it. . . . Who needs additional people when we cannot employ our own citizens?"

After many months of travel through the parts of the United States most affected by immigration, it is clear to me that something big is going on. To see Koreans, Vietnamese, and Cambodians contending for places with the Mexicans, Salvadorans, blacks, and "Anglos" of Los Angeles is to glimpse what New York must have been like when Ellis Island was more than a monument. To examine Miami's recent economic, political, and social history is to see Cuban and Haitian immigration as the event around which all others turn. In countless other places, from Brooklyn to rural Wisconsin, from Houston to Orange, New Jersey, the words heard in the air, the clothes and faces seen on the street, the courses taught in the schools, have all changed because of immigration.

But it is far from clear to me that the changes under way are ominous or bad.

The best-known "facts" about today's immigration are, in many cases, not facts at all. Because of the 808,000 people who were admitted legally in 1980, politicians and authorities have suggested that the U.S. is experiencing an unprecedented foreign flow. A well-respected immigration expert, Michael Teitelbaum, of the Carnegie Endowment for International Peace, has written in *Foreign Affairs* that "immigration and refugee flows to the United States in the late 1970s were at or near the highest levels ever experienced. . . . "

This is hyperbole. The year 1980 was the recent peak. One year later, after the Cuban and Haitian boatlift was over, and after the greatest surge of Indochinese refugees had passed, legal immigration fell to 697,000. By contrast, it was 1.2 million in 1907, and exceeded one million in five other years near the turn of the century. Today's figures do not include illegal immigrants, but the figures from the turn of the century (when there were few illegals) do not include anyone who arrived legally by ship in cabin class or by land, from Canada or Mexico.

Since the American population was so much smaller early in the century, the relative impact of immigration was far greater then. From 1880 to 1890, and again from 1900 to 1910, the average annual flow of counted immigrants was equal to more than one percent of the American population. From 1970 to 1979, it was *one fifth* of one percent. The foreign-born made up 4.7 percent of the population in 1970; they made up 8.8 percent in 1940 and 14.8 percent in 1910.

Many politicians and experts assert that the U.S. is unique in its vulnerability to immigration. Governor Lamm, for example, says that "the unemployed . . . will never get jobs as long as we continue to take in twice as many immigrants as the rest of the world combined." The "twice as many" calculation simply fails to count nearly one million Ethiopian refugees who have fled to Somalia (a nation of 4 million people) and the 1.5 million Afghans displaced into Pakistan. In normal years, the U.S. does admit more immigrants and refugees than any other country, but Canada and Australia have accepted more relative to their population sizes. From 1956 to 1978, the U.S. never received more than 2.8 legal immigrants for each thousand in its population. During the same period, Canada's rate was as high as 17 per thousand, and Australia's rate was as high as 15.1.

Yet statistics are at best a crude indication of people's real concerns about immigration, and a statistical rebuttal is not enough. "It is difficult to explain to residents of the community that the Indochinese refugees are drying skinned cats out on the clothes line because they enjoy cats as a delicacy in their country," the mayor of Santa Ana, California, told a congressional committee in 1981. It is difficult to feel at ease about the impact of the new arrivals, difficult to guess whether the cultural fabric will stretch, as it has before, or finally be torn.

The unspoken question about the immigrants is *What are they doing to us?* Will they divide and diminish the nation's riches? Will they accept its language? Will they alter racial relations? Will they respect the thousand informal rules that allow this nation of many races to cohere?

---

## THE NEW ASIAN IMMIGRANTS[2]

Walking along Broadway on Manhattan's Upper West Side, you glance over at the greengrocer's where you've shopped for years and discover a Korean behind the counter where an Italian used to stand.

[2]Reprint of an article by Robert Lindsey, chief of the *New York Times* Los Angeles bureau. *New York Times Magazine.* p 22+. My. 9, '82. Copyright © 1982 by The New York Times Company. Reprinted by permission.

The 7:56 pulls into the Hartsdale railroad station in West-
chester County, and on some mornings it seems that half of the
commuters who board the train are Japanese businessmen headed
for jobs in New York City, all dressed in the same uniform—a
dark suit, and carrying a leather briefcase.

In California's Silicon Valley, hundreds of Korean and Chinese assemblers hunch over the precision machines that make integrated circuits. A few years ago, their employers farmed out the
same kind of work to Korea and Taiwan.

And in Orange County, California's once legendary red-
white-and-blue homeland for the kooky right wing, there are so
many immigrants from Southeast Asia these days that the schools
have employed specialists who can speak more than a dozen Asian
languages and dialects.

These Asian immigrants are part of a population tide that is
changing the face of America. According to the 1980 Census,
Asians were the fastest growing ethnic group in the United States
during the 1970s, increasing 125 percent to more than 3.5 million.
In the same way that millions of Europeans were propelled across
the Atlantic at the turn of the century by poverty and by political
and racial discrimination, the 1970s sent a torrent of people across
the Pacific—Koreans, Filipinos, Chinese, Thais, Japanese, Vietnamese, Cambodians and other Asians who came to America, like
the Europeans who preceded them, in search of a better life, another chance.

And, the flow may have only just begun.* Some population re-
searchers expect the nation's Asian population to grow at an even
faster rate during the 1980s than it did during the 70s because of
an above-average birth rate in many Asian communities and ac-
celerating immigration—both legal and illegal.

Across Asia, America has become the land of hope and dreams
for millions. But what this influx of Asians will mean to a country
whose culture is deeply rooted in Europe can only be guessed at
now. Even with the recently growing migration, Asians make up
only about 1.6 percent of the nation's population.

*Immigration reform bills were approved by the Senate in 1983 and the House in 1984.

Yet, their influence is already spreading rapidly, from the concert music we listen to, to the foods we eat and how we prepare them, to the clothes we wear, to the way we decorate our homes, to the sense of revitalization that Asians have given to scores of urban communities across the country, to a hard-driving entrepreneurial spirit that America hasn't seen in decades.

Asian immigrants often attempt to embrace Western styles in art and music, leaving behind the cultural heritage of their native countries. But in subtle ways, and perhaps unconsciously, the Asians are beginning to infuse our European cultural legacies with a rich new flavor. The influences range from what a music teacher at the Juilliard School in New York calls a compelling undercurrent in the music played by the growing number of orchestras populated by Chinese and Korean string players, to shadings in our art that could best be characterized by the Japanese word *shibui*—the concept of understated, refined simplicity devoid of extraneous detail.

In much the same way that the relatively small number of European Jews who came to the United States during the last century had an outsized impact on American business, science and culture, the Asians are likely to have an influence on this country far out of proportion to their numbers.

"Some of the similarities between the Asians and the Jews are quite striking," says Arthur H. Rosen, president of the National Committee on United States–China Relations. "There are the same kind of strong family ties and the same sacrificial drive on the part of immigrant parents who couldn't get a college education to see that their children do."

Partly out of fear of the latent prejudice toward Orientals that has erupted periodically throughout American history, Asians who have been here for more than a few years tend to be more assertive politically than many other ethnic minorities. As a group, they are well educated and well informed on political matters and are likely to play a growing role in the governing process. Many of the newest arrivals tend to vote Democratic after gaining citizenship. But there is a strong conservative bent among Asian-American entrepreneurs. Like American businessmen, they possess the attitudes and values that Ronald Reagan exploited in his 1980 Presidential campaign.

The number of Asians who have succeeded and prospered in their new home was illustrated in statistics recently published by the United States Bureau of the Census: Asians had the highest median family income of any ethnic group in the country: $22,075 compared with $19,908 for the nation as a whole. And 75 percent of them were high-school graduates, compared with 69 percent of whites, 51 percent of blacks and 43 percent of Hispanics.

However, there has been a fundamental change in the migration, according to Kevin F. McCarthy, a demographer who has evaluated the Asian immigration to America for the Rand Corporation, a research group in Santa Monica, Calif. Earlier emigrants from both China and Southeast Asia were skilled and ambitious—often, in fact, educated professional people. But there is a second wave of refugees—those who have arrived in the last few years—and they are often unskilled and uneducated, illiterate even in their own language.

Americans confronted with this new tide of immigrants are asking themselves what effects it will have on the economy. The United States, McCarthy points out, has a long tradition of opening its doors to refugees fleeing political oppression. The principal issue to be dealt with in the future, he says, is whether this country can afford to accept millions of immigrants from underdeveloped countries seeking not political refuge, but simply a better life.

Many of the recent refugees, McCarthy explains, appear to be fleeing economic bad times. In some communities Asian refugees are already taxing social services, and there are growing complaints that they are taking jobs from Americans.

A visit recently to some of the communities around the country where the majority of Asians have settled illustrates the many differences among the immigrant groups: The well-to-do businessman from Seoul who sells out his holdings in Korea and flies first-class to Los Angeles with enough cash to buy a $300,000 home and a $500,000 liquor store has little in common with the Hmong tribesman who fled a primitive mountain hamlet in Laos and, after escaping in a crowded boat, comes to America unable to read even in his own language.

Most generalizations about the Asian immigrants are flawed. New stereotypes, like "hard-working" and "obsessed with education," fail just as badly as old ones, like "inscrutable" and "clannish." Still, as you travel around the country meeting the new immigrants in their homes and on the job, a sense quickly emerges that, despite the problems that bedevil them, they comprise a powerhouse of drive and ambition that is likely to have a broad impact on the life of the country.

During the last five years or so, Flushing, Queens, has been transformed by the arrival of tens of thousands of immigrants from Korea, China and the Philippines. Stores owned by Asians line the streets. Real-estate offices have signs outside in both English and Korean; foodstore proprietors sell ethnic foods that are identified in their own language, and restaurants post menus with Oriental characters on one side and English on the other.

"We are new in America and have to work three times harder than you do," says Genghis Kim, a real-estate agent, who arrived in the United States from Seoul 12 years ago and received his bachelor's degree from Rutgers University. "We have to help each other."

Across the continent in Orange County, Calif., Chi Loi, a delicate, waiflike young woman, boasts that she got out of South Vietnam "at the very last minute—really, the last minute"—before the fall of Saigon in 1975. She and her husband, Dong, worked at two jobs each for several years in order to accumulate enough money to buy a fish market, which they opened earlier this year.

"Some Americans don't like us," she said as she scrubbed the shop's floor. "They think we came with gold and diamonds. I try to explain that we're not that kind of people. We work very hard, to save money."

And then, with a smile, she held up her hands to show that they were calloused, as if to rest her case.

Such opportunities have not always been available to Asian immigrants in this country. By and large, Asians of earlier generations who wanted to come to the United States faced harsh immigration laws. If they managed to reach America at all, they faced serious discrimination in the workplace, which, for many, meant relegation to menial jobs in agriculture, restaurants and laundries. In an effort to set up a protective barrier against an alien culture and language, they tended to practice a kind of separatism, isolating themselves with others from their own country.

Participants in the new Asian invasion frequently continue to live together. Many are finding doors still closed and life in America little more than a grim confinement to a sweatshop. But some things are changing. More and more Asians are entering the mainstream of American life and many are achieving positions of leadership in science, business, music, art, architecture, fashion, the theater and other fields.

From Seiji Ozawa, the conductor of the Boston Symphony Orchestra, who came from Japan, to Yo-Yo Ma, the awesome Chinese cellist, to Myung Whun Chung, who grew up in Korea, came to this country to study at Juilliard and went on to become one of this country's most exciting young conductors and pianists, Asians have already become a major component of the classical-music world in America.

Among the more than 1,500 Asian artists said to be working in New York City, painters like Arakawa and Ushio Shinohara, the sculptor Isamu Noguchi and the video-art pioneer Nam June Paik are regarded by some critics as among the best now working in America.

I. M. Pei and Minoru Yamasaki are the best known of many Asian architects at work in this country.

Willa Kim, who grew up in a poor family in Los Angeles's Koreatown, won a Tony award last year for designing the costumes for Broadway's "Sophisticated Ladies." Another Korean, Cathy Hardwick (who married an American before she began her career) is regarded as a major designer of women's sportswear on Seventh Avenue.

The migration has produced entrepreneurs such as Dr. An Wang, the founder of Wang Laboratories, a pioneer in computerized word processing, and Hiroaki (Rocky) Aokie, who created the Benihana of Tokyo restaurant chain. It has also produced executives like Ming Hsu, who came to America from China in the closing days of World War II and began a career that has carried her to a vice presidency of the RCA Corporation. She was recently appointed director of the Division of International Trade for the state of New Jersey.

When Dr. Samuel C. C. Ting, of the Massachusetts Institute of Technology, won the Nobel Prize in Physics in 1976—a year in which all of the Nobels were won by Americans—he delivered his acceptance speech in English, only after giving it first in Chinese—"just for fun," he said, but also to stress his ethnic background. Dr. Ting is one of the more prominent of thousands of Asian scientists and teachers working for industry and in academia in this country.

There are success stories of Asians who came to America and became well known. But there are also countless thousands of other, less dramatic success stories, from mom-and-pop grocery stores to flourishing electronics companies.

Le Thai Hans was transplanted seven years ago from her shattered homeland of Vietnam to an alien culture—the American South. While living in a refugee camp in Thailand, she met a physician from the Center for Disease Control in Atlanta who agreed to sponsor the emigration of her family and to give her a job.

Her husband, Pruyen, a former Vietnamese intelligence officer, spoke no English, and could not get a job immediately. Mrs. Le's salary alone was not enough to support the family, so she began making egg rolls, which she sold during lunch hour to friends at work. A newspaper ran an article about her egg rolls, and business flourished; she now owns two restaurants and an Oriental food market in Atlanta. Her success, she says, was a result of "luck" and of working 16 hours or more a day.

In a comment that seems an echo of immigrant dreams of generations past, and a credo for many of the new Asian immigrants, she says: "I believe with hard work you can get everything you want. You have to be willing to help yourself first."

When finalists for the 1982 Westinghouse Science Talent Search gathered to be honored recently at the Mayflower Hotel in Washington, it seemed to surprise no one that six of the 40 finalists were Asian, even though Asians account for only a tiny percentage of the national population. Figures showing such disproportionate academic success have become commonplace.

At the Juilliard School near Lincoln Center, 15 percent of the enrollment is Asian. And at the Berkeley campus of the University of California, more than 20 percent of the undergraduates these days are Asians, even though they make up only 5.3 percent of the state's population. At major graduate schools of business, such as Harvard and Stanford, there has also been a disproportionate representation of Asian students for almost a decade.

At Stuyvesant High School in New York, one of the most selective high schools in the country, where almost 10,000 applicants competed last year for 750 seats in the freshman class, about 20 percent of the students are Asians, according to Gaspar R. Fabbricante, the principal. What explains the high rate of success?

"I attribute it to culture and family backing," he says. "The Asians seem to have a tradition of scholarship and respect for learning. They have tremendous drive."

One of the Westinghouse finalists, Richard Ke-Jen Chang, a 17-year-old Stuyvesant senior and a Chinese-American who came to this country in 1973, describes the Asian families he knows: "They have a high regard for education, and the parents are willing to sacrifice their lives for the next generation."

Max Watras, who heads the music and art programs at Stuyvesant, says that most Asian students he knows had an uncommon "gift for detail and precision" that makes them particularly effective in mathematics, music and art.

"They not only have a sense of self-discipline but of self-criticism," he says. "They don't follow blindly, but they're willing to accept the demands we place on them. If I told them to memorize a chapter in a history book, they'd know it the next day."

A teacher at the Bronx High School of Science, another highly selective school with a large proportion of Asian students, recounted a conversation she once had with an Asian parent: "He said that when he was younger, he couldn't decide whether he should work in a restaurant or a laundry. He decided that when you work in a restaurant, you're away too many hours. 'If I work in a laundry,' he said, 'I can see my children and ask them: "What did you learn today? Show me what you learned today."' He told me he'd gone to work in a laundry, and he said: 'I got a doctor; I got a lawyer.'"

Asians have long encountered discrimination and exploitation in this country. Indeed, many who have arrived in America in the last 150 years probably wished that they had stayed home.

During the 19th century, thousands of poor Chinese workers were imported to this country to provide cheap labor for construction of the Western railroads. Serfs in all but name, they left a synonym in our language for exploited, underpaid workers: coolie labor. Hundreds, working for pennies a day, died trying to build the railroads. But enough survived to create Chinese communities in San Francisco, Los Angeles, New York and elsewhere, and some of their descendants became merchants and bankers and helped further the trade with China that began in the 19th century.

In later years, sizable numbers of Japanese and Koreans went to the West Coast, mostly to work as farm laborers, although some eventually prospered in business and other fields. In 1924, amid emotional outcries about a "yellow peril," Congress passed the Alien Quota Act, which all but excluded Asians by setting numerical quotas restricting immigration almost exclusively to Europeans.

After Pearl Harbor pushed the United States into World War II, sentiment against Orientals intensified once again, and thousands of Japanese who lived on the West Coast were interned in prison camps.

In 1965, as a kind of an ancillary effect of the civil-rights movement, Congress repealed the 1924 law, and racial quotas were abolished. Would-be migrants from Asia then faced the same restrictions as immigrants from elsewhere—a limitation of 20,000 from each country annually, with an overall limit each year from all countries of 270,000.

The new law opened the door to a new influx of immigrants from Japan, Korea, Taiwan and other countries. The door opened still wider in 1975, when the Government of South Vietnam fell, and the United States agreed to accept hundreds of thousands of refugees from Southeast Asia.

Last year, Congress voted to give mainland China its own quota of 20,000 immigrants a year while retaining the quota for Taiwan, thus effectively giving the Chinese a combined quota of 40,000, the most for any ethnic group.

Social workers and educators who work with the immigrants emphasize that there are major differences between many of the latest arrivals and those who came to America during the early to middle 1970s. Some people who work with the Asian immigrants refer to this group as the Second Wave.

Many, if not most, of those who came shortly after the quota law was abolished were college-trained professionals who brought their families from Taiwan, Korea and Hong Kong; some were well-to-do and able to invest in homes and businesses. Many of the initial Vietnamese refugees who came here after the fall of Saigon had also worked in the professional classes in their own country.

But the more recent immigrants, those from mainland China as well as the "boat people," who fled Cambodia, Laos, rural Vietnam and other Southeast Asian countries, are often poorly educated and unskilled and have no familiarity with English.

Cecilia Chin, a social worker for the Chinese American Service League in Chicago, says that many of the new refugees from mainland China, like many of the Southeast Asian "boat people," are unskilled and illiterate, even in Chinese.

"The Chinese kids from the mainland we are getting are not the same kids as the ones we got from Hong Kong and Taiwan," says a principal in an elementary school in New York's Chinatown. "In terms of productivity, we are finding that the kids who lived under Communism lack motivation. It's really amazing to see the change. It's as if they're telling us: 'We're here now. Make us learn.'"

Nowhere is there more evidence of the influx of Southeast Asian refugees, or the problems and cultural conflicts that they face, than in Orange County, the sprawling suburban megalopolis south of Los Angeles.

More than 50,000 Vietnamese, Laotians and Cambodians have settled in the county, whose population is two million. Orange County's Asians represent more than one-tenth of the total number of Asian refugees who have come to this country since 1975; some were settled there by the Government, others came via so-called secondary migration, a tendency of refugees who are re-settled elsewhere in the country to gravitate to California—and, to some extent, Texas—where the climate is warm and there are already large numbers of refugees.

In Orange County, Asian immigrants have overloaded the public schools and medical facilities—they are blamed for a sharp rise in the rate of tuberculosis and certain other diseases. In addition, there has been growing resentment among some lower-income whites, as well as blacks and Hispanics, who feel that the refugees are taking jobs and housing that would otherwise go to them; and after some refugees admitted to news reporters that they often ate dogs and cats in their native lands, they are blamed whenever a nonrefugee family's pet disappears.

Still, despite such problems, a large number of the refugees are succeeding, often with the help of a large family network.

Dong Loi, who bought the fish market with his wife, owned several stores in Vietnam before coming to this country in 1975; his wife is the daughter of a tailor; they met in this country, married, saved for their store and meanwhile helped arrange passage for her brothers, Nhien and Hiep, who, says Chi Loi, "walked across Cambodia" to make it. Now, the brothers work in the fish market, and they all live with other family members, a total of 10 people in a rented two-bedroom house.

Mrs. Loi says that she worries sometimes about calls from Asian gang members demanding protection payments and she is concerned about the hostility she has felt from some Americans—there was a brief petition drive last year to halt the spread of Vietnamese-owned businesses in the Orange County town of Westminster.

But, she says, despite the hostility and other problems, they are happy to be in America. "We came for freedom," she says.

What is the influx of Asians likely to mean to America?

Asia, of course, has long had an influence on this country, from stirring a fascination with Oriental religions and art a century ago to helping to shape the architecture of Frank Lloyd Wright in the 1930s. For the most part, though, Asia has done more importing of ideas and hardware from the West than it has exported, and we have taken our lead from Europe.

But these days, the Asian presence is pervasive: We drive Datsun automobiles, gather around Sony television sets and dine on Noritake china. Uncounted thousands of us attend karate classes every week. We may even work in an office building owned by an investor in Hong Kong or Tokyo.

When we go out for an Oriental meal, it no longer means just Cantonese-style chop suey or chow mein. We've graduated to more sophisticated styles of Chinese, Japanese, Korean, Thai and other Asian cuisines. In New York alone, at last count, there were 269 Japanese restaurants. Even some of New York's best French chefs admit that there is a subliminal Asian influence in the way they arrange and garnish servings of *nouvelle cuisine,* putting emphasis on the appearance of the food as well as the taste.

Immigrant communities are taking root from Boston to Seattle. In many of these neighborhoods the immigrants are reviving old, deteriorated blocks, like parts of the Lower East Side in New York and fringes of the North Beach section of San Francisco. A stretch of Olympic Boulevard in Los Angeles has become the sparkling center of a Korean community of almost 100,000.

On the North Side of Chicago, Japanese, Korean and Thai merchants have turned a part of Clark Street into a lively, inviting Oriental enclave. In Linda Vista, a section of San Diego, almost a third of the residents—about 7,500—are refugees from Southeast Asia, and some American veterans of the Vietnam War say that there are parts of the community that could have been transplanted in toto from old Saigon.

In Houston, which supports four Asian-language newspapers these days, cattlemen and oil roustabouts are sometimes startled when they approach the city from the south and run across the Crystal Palace Mall, which has a dozen shops, a nightclub and other facilities for Vietnamese refugees.

In these and other cities, the Asians have become significant elements of the local economy.

In Los Angeles and New York, which both have large concentrations of business offices staffed by representatives of Japanese and other Asian countries, the expatriate businessmen, who are generally rotated back to their home offices every three years or so, are credited with injecting millions of dollars into the local economy each year.

The new Asian immigrants are important to the garment, hotel and restaurant businesses. According to the Asian Law Caucus, a rights group in San Francisco, as many as 6,000 Filipino nurses are recruited annually by American hospitals to help alleviate the national nursing shortage.

In the future, as more and more of the Asians who have arrived here since 1968 leave college and move upward in their careers, it is likely that the aptitudes for science, mathematics and business with which many of them are imbued will contribute increasingly to high-technology industries. Ming Hsu, the New Jersey director of International Trade, who came from China after World War II, says that it was very difficult for members of her generation—especially women—to rise in the business world. It should be easier in the future, she says. "But you don't legislate changes in social attitudes; you can't change people's opinion overnight."

The most recent wave of immigrants, she predicted, will probably have more difficulty than the earlier, better-educated immigrants. "They lack some of the initiative, but I think they still have the Asian work ethic. I think they'll play a part in the urban renewal process around the country; they'll live in a ghetto and try to turn it around."

Is the work ethic contagious? Some educators at schools where there are large numbers of high-achieving Asian pupils say they have noticed that the youngsters provide a competitive prod to other students to work harder, but we probably will not know how contagious the Asians' industriousness is in our economy for a few more years.

And although the Asian immigrants are expected to enrich the nation's cultural life, the specific ways in which they may do so are not yet clear. A passion for music, particularly among Chinese

and Korean young people, has led to an explosion in the genesis
of high-quality string players in this country. But the Asian community has not yet produced any top-flight classical singers nor
have the Asians advanced far in musical composition. Still, there
are some people who believe that with so many Asians entering
the American musical scene, it is inevitable that they will leave a
special mark on our music.

At the moment, according to Vincent Persichetti, a distinguished composer and teacher at the Juilliard School, most of the
young Asian musicians are striving to absorb Western musical
culture and perhaps rejecting the music of their homelands. But
he suggests the possibility that there is a subliminal effect surviving their efforts. "I've noticed some of their string players," he
says, "and subconsciously I think some of them are playing an
Asian turn of phrase; they play certain phrases with a dark orange
undercurrent that is quite beautiful."

Only a handful of the Asian artists who have emigrated to
New York have found success so far. Many have to support themselves in menial jobs or are supported by their wives, says Katsko
Suzuki, who came to New York 16 years ago and now owns a
New York gallery that specializes in contemporary Japanese art.
"They're not making it. I tell them, 'Why don't you go back? It's
so much easier in Japan.' But they want to be in New York, because it's the art capital of the world; some go home, some commit
suicide, some keep trying."

American art buyers, she adds, are showing an increasing interest in the work of some Asian artists, but they are confused by
what constitutes "Asian art."

"There is almost universal interest in and acceptance of Asian
principles of art," says Dr. Susan Larsen, an associate professor
of art history at the University of Southern California. "It is subtle. It's not that they're painting bamboo or cherry blossoms; it's
a tendency toward understatement and refinement in their art that
parallels the refinement in modernism; it's the elimination of extraneous detail." And, like others, she expects the influence to
grow.

However, another U.S.C. art historian, Dr. Patricia Berger,
emphasizes that there "is a world of difference" between the art

of China, Japan, Korea and the Philippines, and, over time, each country may affect American artists in its own way. So far, she notes, Japan has had by far the greatest influence in this country, and it ranges from an impact on the design of our furniture and handcrafts to the design of gardens and the use of Japanese-style wood-block art in the preparation of advertisements by McDonald's, the hamburger chain. Indeed, she adds, the Japanese influence "is so integrated we don't even notice it anymore. They have moved into our hearts and we don't even know it."

March Fong Eu, California's Chinese-American Secretary of State, is the state's highest Asian official. She believes that Asian-Americans, as a well-educated, well-informed minority, will probably exercise a political clout in excess of their proportion.

"If you look back over the history of the Asian presence here in America," she said, "the Government hasn't been very kind to us." With the increasing number of Asians in this country, and the growing economic success of many of them, she said, it appears that a new wave of anti-Asian feeling might be developing in parts of the country, where Asian immigrants are being used as "scapegoats" by some unemployed Americans.

But Mrs. Eu believes that Asian groups may be trying to form a political coalition. "There have been several meetings in California with the feeling: 'We all come from different cultures, but we must work together,'" she says.

"I think there's a feeling that if people don't take an interest in politics, and they recede into the background, they may be subject to the same kind of oppression they came from."

## FROM OTHER SHORES[3]

Whether it be New York, Los Angeles, Miami, Houston, or Chicago, the person next to you—on the bus, in the coffee shop, at the movie theater—may not be an American citizen. Instead, there is a good chance that he or she is a recent immigrant—from as far away as Indochina or as near as a Caribbean island.

The new stream of immigrants flowing into America represents a broad cross section of countries from around the world. Like their European and Caribbean predecessors, these expatriates have come to America to seek a better life than their native countries had to offer.

Until 1930, immigration to the United States was almost exclusively a European phenomenon. Then for the following three decades, Latin Americans—mostly Mexicans—comprised 15 percent of the immigrant rolls. By 1970 that portion had swollen to 40 percent, with an influx of Central and South Americans. Since 1980, an estimated 153,000 Haitians and Cubans also have sought refuge in the United States.

Asian countries have provided a significant number of our recent immigrants. Although Chinese and Japanese have been part of the American "melting pot" since the 1800s, during the last two decades, refugees from various other Asian nations have settled on American shores. In the 1970s, Koreans, Filipinos, Taiwanese, and more than 600,000 Indochinese, along with other immigrants from India, Pakistan, and Bangladesh, came here.

The most recent immigration statistics reveal that in 1981, 659,000 immigrants and refugees legally entered the United States, and an estimated 500,000 or more illegally entered.

The House Select Committee on Immigration and Refugee Policy reported that 70 percent of the new immigrants have settled in California, Florida, Illinois, New Jersey, New York, and Texas—six states with large black populations—and are concentrated in key urban areas. Many of these immigrants have established businesses in black communities, while others are directly competing with native Americans for jobs and housing in a recession economy. Angered and frustrated by the growing success of these "intruders," as they are called by some, many black Americans are making accusations of foul play. They charge that the foreigners receive preferential treatment in several ways from the government, including special aid to set up small businesses and priority in jobs established through affirmative action programs. The feeling is that the newcomers are taking away many of the gains in jobs and services that blacks have painfully won through decades of struggle. This argument first took root in the early 1900s when West Indian blacks began coming to the United States and resurfaced in the 1950s and 60s when Mexicans and other Spanish-speaking groups began pouring in. As a result of all this, relations between blacks and the new immigrants show signs of strain.

In Harlem, for example, the relationship between black residents and the Korean merchants is at boiling point. Some black groups are boycotting Korean businesses, charging them with discriminatory hiring practices and a general unresponsiveness to the community. There is a general feeling that these newcomers plan to leave once they have raised enough capital to relocate in more prosperous neighborhoods.

In Compton, a municipality of Los Angeles County that is 80 percent black, Hitachi Consumer Products Co. of America has reached a settlement with California's Fair Employment and Housing Department. The company had been accused of discriminating against blacks by hiring Asians instead. As part of the settlement, the company agreed to pay $250,000 in damages to applicants who had applied for jobs in the disputed period between January and October of 1981 and to initiate an extensive affirmative action hiring program.

"At a time when unemployment is at a record high and with black opportunities being eroded on all fronts, it is difficult to stand up and cheer these new citizens," says John Mack, president of the Urban League in Los Angeles. "Don't get me wrong. Blacks strongly support the fundamental right of others to come to the United States to start a new life. However, our concern is that all of this is being done at the expense of black people. At times it appears that our government leaders give a higher priority to welcoming new immigrants than to helping those folks who are already here."

On the one hand, many black Americans applaud the hard work and long hours these immigrants put in to establish businesses. Other blacks are deeply concerned over the way Caribbean and Hispanic immigrants and undocumented workers, especially in Florida, are being shamelessly exploited in the Southern agricultural labor market.

In many ways, the news media have served to inflame the controversy by headlining conflicts between the groups, regardless of how minor the incidents actually have been. Lloyd Williams, president of the predominantly black Uptown Chamber of Commerce in Central Harlem, points to a CBS affiliate television program, "The People," which was aired 47 times in the metropolitan tri-state area. "The program had no balance," insists Williams, who was interviewed on the show. "It presented the hard-line position held by a few Harlem merchants that Koreans are simply exploiting the community." Williams believes that the feelings of other Harlem businesspeople might have been more favorable to the Koreans, which would have given the program more credibility.

The news media also have been guilty of making unsubstantiated high assessments on the performance and success rate of the immigrants, as compared to the indigenous black and Hispanic population. For example, *Newsweek,* in a recent article "Asian Americans: A 'Model Minority,'" pointed to the burgeoning success of these groups in contrast to certain existing minority populations. Aside from inflaming the tension between blacks and the new immigrants, these comparisons proved very little. What the media fail to report is that most new immigrants arrive with better training and more resources than many indigenous Americans have—black as well as white.

Of the immigrants from Asian countries who reported their occupations, 50 percent were trained in a professional or technical field. When this general statistic is broken down and itemized, 75 percent of the Indians, 50 percent of the Filipinos, 40 percent of the Koreans, and 30 percent of the Japanese and Chinese were in these professional and technical categories. Another 10 percent of the Asian immigrants were managers and administrators (18.8 percent of the Japanese, 16.8 percent of the Chinese, 11.6 percent of the Koreans, and 6 percent of the Filipinos and Indians).

According to Professor Setsuko Nishi of the City University of New York, the 1975 US immigration report reveals that "almost two-thirds of the Asian immigrant workers bring . . . a very high level of occupational experience as professionals, technicians, managers and administrators."

The immigrants who arrived in the late 1960s and early 70s were often members of the middle class in their native countries. As former merchants, skilled workers, and crafts people, they came to the United States with adequate job training, good business experience, and even some capital raised from the sale of property in their home country.

It is not the skilled immigrants, however, who are causing most of the concern in the black communities. The controversy revolves around the less educationally advantaged immigrants who have established a presence in the black community. The so-called "boat people"—Indochinese, Cubans, and Haitians—came in full flight from oppressive political regimes and intolerable economic conditions in their countries. Most of these people come to the United States with minimal job skills and with no possessions beyond what they could carry.

In Washington, D.C., Koreans own over 300 businesses, most of them situated in black neighborhoods. On 125th Street in Harlem, Koreans own 58 stores, nearly all opened in the last few years. In other black neighborhoods, new business owners are often Arab, Indian, or Indochinese. Notes one black Harlem resident ruefully, "Everyone's doing business in the black community except black people."

"In New York, the midtown and downtown commercial areas are saturated," says John Edwards Jr., former general manager of the New York State Harlem Urban Development Corporation. "The logical growth area in the city is Harlem, and growth is taking place. A lot of people want a piece of Harlem now."

Certainly, the Koreans are among these. Won Duck Kim, owner of the Guy & Gal clothing store on 125th Street, chose to open his business in Harlem because of the low rent and the scarcity of clothing stores in the area. Kim pays $1,275 a month for a 5000-square-foot space—a steal when compared to the $5,000 and $6,000 rents asked by midtown Manhattan landlords.

Are these Koreans displacing black businesses, as critics of the new immigrants are prone to argue? Mal Locus, the black owner of Harlem's Rainbow Music, and president of the 125th Street Business Association, insists that the Koreans have merely filled a void. Locus points out that numerous stores on 125th Street had remained vacant after former owners, many of whom were white, moved out of the area. As victims of racism and bureaucracy, black entrepreneurs were often denied loans from banks to start their own establishments. Won Duck Kim points out that he and other immigrant Korean entrepreneurs explored the entire city before settling uptown.

There is no mystery to what the Koreans and other immigrant businessmen are doing. They are finding niches that were overlooked or not available to others. The immigrants from Bangladesh, for example, have moved *en masse* into inexpensive ethnic restaurants; many Indians, especially those of Gujerati ancestry, have purchased motels in New Jersey and Florida as well as on the West Coast. Similarly, the Koreans have established themselves in newsstand, fresh produce, and grocery businesses.

Locus notes that although the Koreans have formed their own business group in Harlem, 21 of them have also become part of the 125th Street Business Association. "They pay dues like everyone else," he points out. And Williams expresses his sympathy, saying, "They are sincere in their efforts to be a part of the community." This observation may be questionable, however, because very few of these store owners in Harlem or in black communities around the country ever move into the neighborhoods where they set up shop. Some blacks also feel that the Koreans are not willing to make a long-term commitment to do business in their communities.

Many blacks are incredulous at the ability of the new immigrants to obtain capital, when blacks have such difficulty. Some wonder if the United States or a foreign government provides financial assistance. Others go so far as to claim that Rev. Sun Myung Moon (the Korean evangelist) and his Unification Church finance the new Korean businesses. Also, there has been speculation as to whether financing from organized crime has been filtering into these businesses.

Despite these doubts and suspicions, there is no tangible proof that any government—domestic or foreign—or any private organization has provided financial aid for any refugee or immigrant business. Officials at the Small Business Administration and at the American Association of MES-BIC's deny that there are new or existing government programs catering exclusively to immigrants. Also, many foreign governments impose severe currency restrictions on emigrants. Koreans are allowed only $2,500; Indians and Pakistanis even less. Nevertheless, many who leave their country buy dollars on the illegal currency market—often at exorbitant exchange rates—and thus smuggle out large sums of cash.

Take the example of Harlem store owner, Won Duck Kim. He arrived in New York in 1970 with his wife, and both quickly found jobs—he in a nursing home, she in a bakery. After nearly eight years of working, the couple had saved about $15,000. Combined with the $25,000 they had received from selling their home in Korea, they had enough capital to start their own business.

Kim explains that he chose clothes merchandising because a couple of Korean clothing wholesalers recommended it. "Without their help, I wouldn't have known what to do," he says. As a rule Asian and Indian merchants favor businesses in which there is a strong vertical network of fellow countrymen.

There is no doubt that the presence of new immigrants, as well as a large group of undocumented workers, has caused some instability in the American labor market. To many, the question is how much. The presence of Asian laborers in Compton, Calif., could have biased the Japanese firm of Hitachi to hire them in preference to the local available black labor. Furthermore, some Japanese workers migrated to the United States with Japanese companies. According to former city manager Ronald Nelson, black unemployment in the city has ranged from 20 to 46 percent in recent years. To rectify this problem, the city of Compton established an industrial park, with warehouses for Sony Corporation, Sanyo Inc., Craig of America, and Hitachi Consumer Products.

"We were happy to get these companies to locate here, but unfortunately they took little initiative in hiring blacks from the community," notes Nelson. It is true, however, that no formal negotiations or contracts were initiated by the community which would require the corporations to do this. The upshot is that Hitachi has been accused of hiring Asians and illegal aliens from neighboring areas. "They [Asians and illegals] worked for less and didn't want to unionize," comments Compton City Councilman Maxey Filer. "Because these groups are here and willing to work at substandard wages, blacks cannot find work." Nevertheless, says the acting city manager, Laverta Montgomery, these corporations have generated $5 million in taxes for the city, which is providing funds for essential revitalization projects.

In Florida, where many Haitians are working in orange groves as pickers, the displacement of American blacks again is an issue. According to Yves Savain, project director for the Phelps Stokes Fund's Haitian Adult Development Education Program (HADEP), the Haitians are working at jobs which are no longer wanted by many black Americans, but are sought by refugees and illegals. It is to be noted in this connection that the piece rates offered by orchard owners translate into a less than minimum wage.

Those new immigrants who come to the United States with a minimum of skills tend to move toward three specific job areas—restaurants, garment manufacturing, and health care—says Charles Keeley of New York's Population Council. There is little evidence that blacks have been displaced in any of these areas, however. Immigrants and undocumented workers work long hours in horrendous conditions, without overtime compensation.

In the health-care field, where many Caribbean and Hispanic immigrants have found work, there is little evidence that any black Americans have been displaced. "These newer workers haven't taken anyone's job away," explains Talbert King of Local 1199, which represents over 80,000 health-care workers in the New York area. King notes that blacks have settled in the technical areas, such as laboratory and radiology, while the new immigrants have gravitated toward more manual jobs in hospitals. Even in nursing, which has experienced a massive Filipino influx, there is no fear of displacement, argues King. "There's such a need for trained personnel in the area that any kind of person with the right skills can find a job."

The influx of the new immigrant groups has created pressures on housing as well. Recent events in Houston may lend credence to the widely held belief that much of the housing in black areas is being bought up or rented by new immigrant groups. The competition for low-cost housing in Houston has led to large-scale conflicts between Vietnamese and blacks in the city's Allen Parkway housing complex. The project has always had a long waiting list, but the trouble began when Vietnamese applicants secured housing ahead of many blacks who had applied earlier.

Black City Councilman Anthony Hall claims that the Allen Parkway episode was an isolated incident, but he emphasizes that shortages are bound to create conflicts among those who have been deprived. The incidents around the housing complex gradually subsided, notes Ron Luce, director of the Houston YMCA Refugee Program, and an uneasy peace exists between the two groups.

In Florida, however, where there has been a sudden influx of Haitian and Cuban refugees, the black housing projects have not been affected. Ron Frazier, a black architect and chairman of the Miami-Dade Chamber of Commerce feels that the tale of displacement is a myth and that the Haitians are merely crowding into the worst of the worst.

There is no doubt that new immigrants are forcing schools to provide additional services—either in the form of English as a Second Language (ESL) or remedial courses. In fact, federal law mandates that schools with certain proportions of non-English-speaking students (or students whose native language is not English) must provide ESL classes. Claire Press, spokeswoman for Louis Armstrong Junior High School in New York City, says that most schools receive additional funds for such programs.

Although the schools do receive additional funding to help provide ESL services, Bernard Steinberg, principal of PS 145 in New York, feels that the school's resources have been stretched to the limit. Other services have invariably been diluted and "the dilution is affecting everyone, not just blacks," Steinberg adds.

It may be inevitable that the arrival of the new immigrants has instilled new fears in black Americans. The relationship between new immigrants and blacks is often strained, with both sides harboring animosity and resentment toward the other. How black communities will be affected by this growing antagonism, especially between Asians and blacks, is of growing concern to many black community leaders. Williams and others believe that if something is not done soon to bring people together, even more conflict will arise.

Part of the blame for the mounting problem must lie with the US government and the new immigrants, argues Khanh Vo, a Vietnamese social worker who has dealt with immigrant groups in Houston as well as in New York. "The Indochinese don't really want to associate with blacks," says Vo. "They have not interacted in the social sense." He believes that many of the government-run refugee orientation programs have fostered racial distinctions, thus making the Indochinese distrust blacks. "They have been told in numerous ways that blacks are not part of the solution. That they are the problem."

Williams agrees that the attitude of the immigrants toward blacks is often culpable. "Sometimes they are their own worst enemy," he says. "New merchants in black communities can't hire black people just to sweep floors and feel that's enough. Any business person—white, Korean, or black—who comes into Harlem and disrespects black people should not be here." Still, Williams and many others contend that blacks are often at fault. To relieve the tensions and guarantee the resurgence of black communities, he says, blacks must begin to work with the new immigrants.

"There must be unity in planning the revitalization of our communities," Williams explains. "The newcomers must understand that they can make for good relations by supporting established black institutions, and blacks must realize that the new merchants are not necessarily taking away opportunities."

Mack expresses a similar view: "One of the unfortunate problems of this divisiveness is that we are having difficulty focusing on the real problems," he says. Mack views the unity of the groups as leverage which could force the government to play a more positive role in educating the new immigrants about the black community.

This issue underscores another, more fundamental problem that must be confronted by the depressed black communities where empty and underutilized stores line the shopping districts. These shops represent potential sources of economic power for our communities—and for the families who are willing to sacrifice good times and leisure hours to make them profitable. If black communities do not organize to seize these entrepreneurial opportunities, no amount of "immigrant education" or "government regulation" will fill the void. Blacks have organized before, and they will have to organize again to give the proposed truce a chance to work.

## II. THE IMPACT OF ILLEGALS

## EDITOR'S INTRODUCTION

The stream of illegal immigrants, mostly Hispanics, who entered the United States in the 1950s and '60s turned into a flood in the 1970s and '80s. Spurred by Central America's uncertain politics, troubled economies, and rapidly expanding labor force, as many as two million Mexicans, Hondurans, Salvadorans, and others may illegally cross the United States border in 1984. As many as five million illegal immigrants may already be in the United States, but no one is sure of the true number. Most illegals find temporary, usually seasonal, work and then return to their home countries, but many others seek permanent residence. These form an exploited underclass, unprotected by law, drawing on government services, and affecting the national economy to an unknown degree.

In the first selection, from *U.S. News & World Report,* William Chaze surveys the difficulties that the U.S. Immigration and Naturalization Service faces in trying to stem the tide of illegal immigrants slipping through the so-called "tortilla curtain" along the Texas-Mexico border. Chaze claims that illegal laborers, willing to work hard in substandard conditions for minimal wages, are displacing many Americans who compete for the same jobs.

The second selection, from *Business Week,* contends that illegal immigration actually strengthens the economy, boosting overall industrial growth by keeping wages down and thereby helping to create as many new jobs for Americans as the immigrants themselves take away. The article acknowledges, however, that some segments of the population, notably blacks and youths, may be hurt disproportionately by competition with illegal immigrants.

## INVASION FROM MEXICO: IT JUST KEEPS GROWING[1]

Propelled by Mexico's worsening economic crisis, a flood of illegal aliens in unparalleled volume threatens to overwhelm the thin green line of the U.S. Border Patrol.

Thousands are slipping each day across the 2,000-mile-long boundary, alone or aided by smugglers charging up to $1,200 a head for rides to Chicago and other cities. The chief magnet: Minimum-wage jobs that pay at least six times the going rate in Mexico because of the peso's devaluation.

In January alone, 83,811 aliens were caught along the border—up 46 percent over the same time a year ago. But by the Border Patrol's own estimate, only 1 in 3 is being apprehended, and even those stopped and sent back often keep trying until they make undetected crossings.

If the agency's reckoning is correct, 2 million Mexicans may sneak into the U.S. before 1983 is over—more than any year in history. About a third can be expected to become permanent residents, on top of an estimated 3 to 6 million Mexican illegals already in the United States. The rest will move back and forth across the border as day workers.

"The flow is unprecedented," says a Border Patrol spokesman. "But the disturbing thing is that this isn't even our peak season. Traffic will pick up in spring. We could see a million apprehensions before the year is out. We may now be seeing just the stream before the flood."

Impact on the U.S. of the wave of undocumented workers is beyond calculation. The surge occurs at a time of the highest American unemployment in four decades and as governments at all levels are hard pressed to provide even for citizens.

Former Secretary of Labor Ray Marshall estimates that joblessness could be halved by shutting off the flow of illegals and deporting those already here.

[1]Reprint of a magazine article by William L. Chaze, staff writer. *U.S. News & World Report.* 94:37+. Mr. 7, '83. Copyright © 1983, U.S. News & World Report, Inc.

## Face-Off on the Rio Grande

The dilemma of a developing nation living next door to one of the world's richest countries comes to life in places such as El Paso, across the Rio Grande from a mean Juárez slum known as Arroyo Colorado. Gaunt and raggedly dressed people carrying a few belongings in sacks poise for a dash to American soil. Found there at any hour of day or night, they wait only for the right moment to make their run for what they hope is a decent, if not prosperous, life.

On one cold, bright February morning, some 100 young men and women stood silently on the Mexican side intently watching—and being watched by—a handful of green-uniformed Border Patrolmen. After a 45-minute standoff, most of the officers departed to attend to other parts of the so-called tortilla curtain fence separating El Paso from Juárez. It was then that the patient Mexicans split up and began quickly crossing up and down the river.

Some are caught by the Border Patrol's rear guard as they sprint through nearby freight yards. Others are arrested crossing a highway leading west toward the Florida Mountains and New Mexico. But for each arrest, others make it to south El Paso's crowded and anonymous barrios.

"Sometimes you feel like a highway patrolman," says Border Patrol agent Leo Aguirre. "He gives a few tickets, but he goes home every night knowing how many speeders are out there. It can be very, very frustrating for a Border Patrolman in a situation like this."

Those caught offer the same story. "There is little work at home," explains Manuel Ortega, 20, a baker caught in a sweep near El Paso. "And when there is a job, the pay is no good for one with a family. Many in my village are coming north." Adds Juan Valasquez, 19, who made it through from the state of Tabasco: "Getting stopped is no big deal. You take the bus back, hang around Juárez near the railroad yards, talk to people, find out about a better spot and then you are across." Picked up three times before he finally made it, Valasquez works in a Las Cruces, N.M., café while saving to join relatives in Lincoln, Nebr.

Showing signs of increasing desperation, the illegals risk all to cross the border. It has become routine for the Border Patrol to find Mexicans mangled by freight trains they try to board in El Paso's Alfalfa rail yards, or else dead of exposure from lying in bitter cold in the sandy river bed. Others are killed by Mexican *bandidos* who waylay them in the brushy no man's land between west El Paso and the river.

"They don't know what they're doing and lose arms and legs and get all chewed up trying to catch freight cars," reports Border Patrolman Mike Calvert. "They grab a coupling and, when the train slows, lose a hand, maybe a leg or worse. Or they get pinned and crushed when oil-field pipes suddenly shift in a gondola car."

Still others risk being killed by El Paso's heavy expressway traffic while running across the road paralleling the border fence. As Calvert patrolled south El Paso, he saw one young man go under the fence and run headlong toward a Mesa Street blood bank where aliens swap blood for cash needed for the long trip north.

When the Mexican saw Calvert's patrol car come squealing around a corner, he turned and, looking neither left nor right, ran into traffic. A car grazed him, but the man limped back through the fence. He could easily have been killed. Says a white-faced Calvert: "You have to feel for them. If they're willing to die like this, it ain't worth the chase."

### *"Soon We'll All Be Here"*

Despite all its efforts, the Border Patrol seems more nuisance than deterrent. "They waste their time," scoffs Juan Martinez, 24, as he drinks beer in an El Paso café. "They make arrests but miss others. My whole family will come next month. Soon we'll all be here."

The Border Patrol's main problem is that it is outmanned. While it has 2,300 agents on the border—covered by an 111-million-dollar budget—no more than 300 are on duty at a time because of rotating shifts and vacations. With a force smaller than the Baltimore Police Department, the El Paso station's 380 agents must cover 85,000 square miles of desert and mountains. Often, a dozen will be spread across the always busy 10-mile strip between El Paso and Juárez. "It sometimes seems Washington really doesn't want us to do the job," comments a veteran patrolman. "We do our best, but there aren't enough of us."

The agency tries to compensate with advanced technology. In Chula Vista, Calif., for instance, hillsides and canyons are mined with magnetic and seismic sensors that signal the presence of man or machine. When a sensor picks up footsteps, an alert is bleeped to a computer at sector headquarters atop a hill overlooking the border. The computer automatically prints out the sensor number, type, location and number of aliens traversing the area.

New infrared scopes used at Chula Vista can home in on body warmth in pitch-darkness. Four-wheel-drive trucks, all-terrain vehicles and trail bikes extend the patrol's reach into rugged canyons. Even so, officials believe twice as many agents would be needed to seal off the border.

"We may be catching more aliens today, but that's because more are coming," says Chula Vista chief Gene Wood. "With all the new technological advances and increased manpower, we are lucky if we are catching as many percentagewise as we did back in the 1950s."

The border itself is hardly more than a line on a map. The Mexicans do not patrol their side, and the Rio Grande at El Paso often is only knee-deep. The few miles of fencing the U.S. has erected is full of holes and in places trampled flat.

One of the most popular crossing points is practically under the Border Patrol's nose at the Paso del Norte Bridge in El Paso. There, an alien has only to drop through a hole in the fence yards from the customs station and run through adjoining Chamizal Park. As Border Patrolman Aguirre changed a tire in the park recently, he looked up and saw a Mexican do just that. The alien disappeared into nearby neighborhoods—like countless thousands before him. "It is so easy to cross," notes Aguirre. "If you are determined, you can do it."

## The 25-Cent Border Toll

Mostly, the U.S. depends on inhospitable terrain—thousands of miles of desert and mountains—to discourage crossings. Traffic across the river is so heavy that enterprising Mexicans have painted offers on the rocks to carry across all comers for 25 cents.

"It can be very dangerous to cross the desert at night and not know where you are going," says Assistant Border Patrol Chief Ray Reaves of El Paso. "That's why so many come across at El Paso and Chula Vista. It's safer. The worst thing that happens is you get caught. But in the desert, you may end up dead—and it is not a pleasant death, either."

With the border as porous as it is, the real challenge for aliens is to get inland—not so easy given the heavy Border Patrol presence at airports, bus and train stations and highway checkpoints. Increasingly, aliens bent on going north must pay smugglers to help them on their way.

The patrol recently cracked several big smuggling rings and obtained convictions, but the trade keeps growing. In a grimy part of Juárez, for instance, expensively dressed Mexicans in cream-colored Stetsons, fancy shirts and hand-tooled boots stand outside the El Viajero Hotel soliciting customers. In nearby Pepe's Cantina, it is simple to buy a forged American driver's license and Social Security card.

The rising tide of illegal aliens has become a major worry for U.S. officials. No one really knows how much aliens cost taxpayers, but some experts believe the figure runs into hundreds of millions of dollars, perhaps billions. A Supreme Court ruling guarantees children of illegal immigrants a free education, and officials are not allowed to ask about a pupil's citizenship status. Result: The state of Texas spends more than 85 million dollars each year to educate 61,000 children of illegal aliens. Last year, nearly 1 in 4 students in the public schools of Brownsville was foreign born.

"Every year, we pick up 800 or 900 students enrolled in Mexican schools the previous year," reports Vidal Treviño, schools superintendent in Laredo. "And we are going to have more of those students as conditions worsen in Mexico."

Los Angeles officials estimate that annual education costs for children of undocumented workers run as high as 415 million dollars. Immigration officials say tens of thousands of alien children are enrolled in schools in Chicago and New York. Scores of American cities now have bilingual-education programs for children illegally in the country.

Costs go beyond schooling. Los Angeles spent 76 million dollars last year on health care for undocumented aliens. Officials estimate that 1 of every 5 patients in the Los Angeles County hospital system is an illegal alien. New York authorities say the state spends up to 12 million dollars a year on health care for illegals.

A study by the Federation for Immigration Reform, a Washington-based group that favors tighter border controls, asserts that aliens today are finding it relatively easy to obtain welfare and unemployment benefits with forged documents. The Immigration and Naturalization Service supports that conclusion, with a study of its own estimating that the total cost in jobless benefits to illegal aliens in Illinois alone could hit 66 million dollars a year.

"The alien-registration card—which says you are lawfully admitted for permanent residence—is the most counterfeited of all government documents," says James Hardin, a Denver INS official. "If you have one, you're entitled to social-service benefits and can even get student aid."

Crime by illegal entrants is a growing worry, some communities report. More arrested undocumented immigrants are found to be armed. Public demands for a crackdown erupted in January when a Mexican who had been deported five times was charged with killing a Dallas policeman.

### The Fight for Jobs

Of all the issues involving illegal aliens, the most controversial is jobs. Those backing tighter immigration laws argue that, for every alien who enters the country illegally, an American worker is displaced. Hispanic groups and others retort that jobs taken by aliens are ones Americans do not want—as day laborers, busboys and workers in garment sweatshops paying less than the minimum wage.

Labor leaders contend that rising U.S. unemployment has changed the picture and that many Americans are now willing to take any kind of job. "From one end of the country to the other, local trade-union leaders report that illegal immigrants are taking jobs from American workers," asserts Jack Sheinkman, secretary-treasurer of the Amalgamated Clothing and Textile Workers Union.

Labor leaders cite INS raids last spring on 560 work sites in nine major cities. The 5,440 illegals arrested were earning an average of $4.81 per hour; some, $12. Surveys since show that 50 percent of those deported from some cities have since found their way back to the U.S.

"It isn't so much that illegal aliens are making inroads into the adult work force as squeezing out kids who would take these jobs to get started," says Hardin of the INS in Denver. "Illegal aliens are some of the best workers in the world, and once an employer starts using them, he gets hooked."

The Border Patrol is convinced that it can never do its job effectively unless Congress enacts tough sanctions against employers who hire illegals. Such a measure died in the House last year after passing in the Senate. It was introduced again in mid-February, but chances for passage are considered only fair.

"About the only way you can secure the border is to hire enough agents to stand hand in hand along the U.S. side," says Assistant Border Patrol Chief Reaves. "Even if you do that, they eventually will get across. This is where the jobs are."

---

## ILLEGAL IMMIGRANTS:
## THE U.S. MAY GAIN MORE THAN IT LOSES[2]

---

Deep down in their hearts, Americans may believe that the nation's doors should be open to anyone who wants to come here and work. After all, most U.S. citizens are descended from immigrants. But a flood of illegal aliens, especially from Mexico, has ignited

[2] Reprint of an article by *Business Week* reporters. Reprinted from the May 14, 1984 issue of *Business Week* by special permission, © 1984 by McGraw-Hill, Inc.

fears that more and more Americans will lose their jobs or at the very least see their wages depressed as a result of immigration. Congress is considering a bill, sponsored by Senator Alan K. Simpson (R-Wyo.) and Representative Romano Mazzoli (D-Ky.), that would legalize the status of illegals already here while clamping down on future illegal entry. The bill has a good chance of passing.*

Unquestionably, there are social and economic costs to illegal immigration. But new economic evidence suggests that, on balance, the nation benefits more from the increased economic growth and lower inflation stemming from illegal immigration than it loses in jobs, lower wages, and welfare costs.

Hard data on illegals are, of course, difficult to come by. Based on the recent surge in arrests of aliens, however, their numbers are growing. The Census Bureau estimates that there are now 5 million to 7.5 million illegal residents, who may be holding between 4 million and 6 million jobs.

While this seems like a huge number, many are jobs for which Americans do not compete. Some illegals are employed in agriculture, picking strawberries and tomatoes in 100° heat. Others hold such urban jobs as dishwashers, busboys, maids, and sewing-machine operators—unattractive to many Americans and therefore difficult for employers to fill. Michael J. Piore of the Massachusetts Institute of Technology argues that there is in effect a "two-tier" labor market in which low-skilled immigrants take unwanted jobs so that little displacement of American workers occurs.

Most experts, however, agree that illegals compete for some jobs that Americans want. The Immigration & Naturalization Service has found illegal aliens working in the garment and food-processing industries in California, casinos in Atlantic City, and electronics companies in Silicon Valley. Indeed, a 1979 government study estimated that one in five jobs held by an alien—in total, as many as 1.2 million jobs—could be filled by unemployed Americans. Those who are especially hurt by competition from illegals are low-skilled workers, primarily minorities and young people.

*Versions of the bill passed the Senate in 1983 and the House in June 1984.

## Selective Samples

However, even 1.2 million jobs represents less than 1% of the total number in the economy. Moreover, that figure is calculated by looking only at the kinds of jobs where immigrants and Americans are most likely to compete. It fails to consider the spur to economic growth that immigration has generated over a long period of time. Illegal immigration, say most economists, has added to the nation's output. This increase in goods and services has created other jobs that have in good part offset the job loss to Americans from direct competition with illegals.

Indeed, many economists view immigration as they do international trade. While the nation as a whole benefits from free trade, uncompetitive industries and their employees can be hurt. Similarly, says Morgan O. Reynolds of Texas A&M University, "open immigration provides net gains for the economy by expanding output and lowering prices, but some people lose."

At the current pace of illegal immigration, which the Census Bureau estimates adds 500,000 people per year, the impact on future unemployment is likely to be quite small. Even if all of those are workers, Data Resources Inc. calculates that it would add only one-tenth of a percentage point to the unemployment rate. The impact on specific regions, such as the Southwest and Florida, would also be modest, says senior economist Elisabeth Allison. The DRI regional models show that higher immigration in these regions will drive up the unemployment rate, but only briefly. Allison explains that people in other states respond to increased immigration by deciding not to move there. This limits the labor force and curbs unemployment.

Such findings do not refute the contention that illegal immigrants drive down wages. Many illegals, for example, are paid less than the minimum: Sheldon L. Maram of California State University found that 21.8% of the illegal restaurant workers he studied were paid less than the minimum wage, compared with 8.4% of the legal workers. Since employers can threaten to report illegals to the authorities, illegals are more likely than others to work for less than the legal minimum wage and put up with sweatshop conditions.

Yet a study by Barton A. Smith of the University of Houston and Robert Newman of the University of British Columbia shows that the effect of lower wages paid to illegals may not be as severe as it seems at first, at least in certain areas. Smith and Newman compared the wages in towns in Texas near the Mexican border, where many illegals live, with towns farther from the border. The average wages in the border cities were 30% to 40% lower than in the more distant areas. But Smith and Newman found that real wages—wages adjusted for the cost of living in each area—were at most only 8% lower. Says Smith: "From the worker's point of view, what he's concerned about is the real wage." Smith believes that lower wages explain part, but not all, of the lower cost of living in the border areas.

## Saved from Extinction

Lower wage costs can have other beneficial effects. For one thing, they tend to keep overall prices low. Lower-paid illegal aliens in agriculture help hold down the prices of fresh fruits and vegetables. More important, low wages allow industries facing severe foreign competition to survive. Without lower wages, some industries—such as the garment industry and consumer electronics—would have to go overseas to compete. Says Yale economist Jennifer Roback: "As long as we have international trade, American industry will compete with low-wage workers. It may be better to employ them here than overseas." Despite the benefits of lower prices and the bolstering of otherwise endangered domestic industries, lower wages may lower U.S. productivity. Dale W. Jorgenson of Harvard believes that low-wage labor slows down the growth of capital spending and thus dampens productivity growth. More cheap labor from Latin America "could undermine to a certain extent the capital spending boom we anticipate in the 1980s," he says. Jorgenson points to a similar slowdown in productivity in the 1970s, which he attributes in part to the swollen labor force that reflected the baby boom and new female workers. Indeed, former Labor Secretary Ray Marshall notes that when child labor was abolished in the late 19th century, the garment industry invested in labor-saving equipment. This ultimately in-

o reduce or eliminate the situations in which entire
re forced to look to other countries for the minimum
decent life.

specially evident as we recognize the growing difficul-
refugee-receiving countries, including our own, face
g refugees. Even where refugee movements take place
ographic region they can have severe impact on the lo-
ions and on economic development. The impact can be
at if refugees are moved to distant third countries. The
adaptation of some refugees should not obscure the
that the refugee experience imposes on all concerned.
n of refugee problems must start with a recognition of
to come to grips with the root causes.

uld be stressed that America's leadership role does not,
cases, require that refugees be admitted to the United
considered approach to refugee programs worldwide has
possible in the past 2 years to reduce substantially the
s of refugees for whom resettlement in the United States
her third countries is the appropriate solution. This has
major U.S. policy objective, one that is supported by the
igh Commissioner for Refugees (UNHCR) and by the in-
ional community as a whole.

prevention is the best cure for a refugee problem, then the
best, clearly, is for refugees to be enabled to return freely to
homelands. Often this cannot take place right away, but in
the factors that caused refugees to flee may change enough
ake possible such voluntary repatriation. We have supported
efforts wherever proposed by the UNHCR, always insisting
t there be safeguards to assure that the refugees' rights are pro-
ted.

Even if voluntary repatriation is not immediately in sight, it
akes sense to care for refugees within their region. In many cases
ighboring countries have ties of language or ethnic character
hich ease the acceptance of refugees and facilitate their longer
rm integration. Such local resettlement also preserves the possi-
ility of the refugees returning eventually to their homelands as
conditions change. In general, the expectation needs to be challenged that becoming a refugee equates to distant emigration. Ex-

creased productivity in the industry and lowered prices. And
Philip L. Martin of the University of California at Davis contends
that the use of aliens in agriculture is holding back important
mechanization.

To some extent, however, the substitution of cheap labor for
capital will also be moderated by an expanding economy. Michael
L. Wachter of the University of Pennsylvania notes that low-
skilled workers may be substitutes for capital, but the increased
output they produce also spurs capital investment.

### Welfare Worries

Even those who recognize that the economic benefits of illegal
immigrants outweigh the negatives worry that legalizing their status could be costly. They fear that illegals who currently are afraid
to seek welfare and jobless benefits will demand them once they
gain amnesty, as the Simpson-Mazzoli bill provides. The Office
of Management & Budget estimates that welfare costs could go
up as much as $10 billion over a three-year period. Concern over
this steep increase helps explain the Reagan Administration's failure to endorse the bill.

But this problem, too, may be less severe than OMB expects.
It appears that illegals already use welfare programs to a greater
degree than previously thought. David Heer of the University of
Southern California compared families of workers in Los Angeles
County. He found that about the same percentage of families of
illegal Mexican workers obtained food stamps and aid to depen-
dent children as did families of Mexican legal immigrants and
American citizens of Mexican descent.

Similarly, David S. North of the New TransCentury Foundation in Washington, D.C., found that aliens do receive unemployment benefits. Of 147 illegals arrested by federal authorities in
1975 who re-entered the labor force, 35% received unemployment
benefits at some time over the next five years.

Thus, if illegal immigrants are legalized, the number demanding more social services could be far less than expected. In general,
fears that a tide of immigrant aliens will wreak economic havoc
seem overstated.

## III. "WRETCHED REFUSE"

## EDITOR'S INTRODUCTION

The line dividing refugee from immigrant is often a fine one. Refugees are those fleeing temporary danger or oppression who intend to return once the danger is past. But, once in their host countries, many refugees never return, and therefore become immigrants. This is especially true of refugees who may have a moral claim on the nation of sanctuary. The 600,000 Vietnamese refugees who permanently entered the United States after the fall of Saigon are a case in point, as, to a lesser extent, are the Mariel boat people deported by Cuba in 1980. As refugees are given special consideration in world law and in national immigration policies, the decision about who is a legitimate refugee and who is an immigrant can pose ethical and political problems for the host country. Are Haitians who apply for entry into the United States economic and political refugees escaping an oppressive rightist regime, and thus worthy of a humanitarian welcome (as they themselves claim), or are they simply trying to avoid unpleasant but bearable conditions under a government firmly allied to the United States, and thus not definable as refugees (as U.S. officials currently maintain)? The plight of those Haitians who managed to enter the country (most were held for long periods in squalid detention camps) has been an international embarrassment to the United States.

In this section's first article, Edward J. Derwinski, a senior State Department official, details the global refugee situation as defined by the United States and explains U.S. entry quotas for the major regions affected. Derwinski's description of current policy as "generous and humane" is questioned by Frank Moan in the second selection; Moan, director of the Office of Jesuit Refugee Services, suggests that the quota system is discriminatory and that the United States sets limits for refugee admission that it never intends to fulfill. Gerda Bikales, a member of the Federation

The Problem of Immigra

for American Immigratio.
from the *Humanist* that ne
fy refugee policy. In her vie
is needed to protect the Unit
and refugees.

## PROPOSED REFUGEE A

Few subjects are of greater hur
cy than the plight of the world's rei
half century has its record of refugee
sion. In this decade alone we have w
a historic scale: 1.6 million refugees
from Ethiopia; and over 3 million from
costs of such exoduses can be measured
home country, often including the able
burden of added population to the rece
near or far, and the human toll on the r

As in the past, the countries from wh
of refugees have fled are those that fall
nation or leadership, for it is in those count
rations of life—which we sum up in the ter.
most persistently violated.

As we look to the future there is growin
need for a full international process of burden
gees. Such a process needs to look for new ways
cle of countries prepared to assist in caring for
need to consider what can be done to anticipate
gee flows, in particular to reduce the size and dur
sive exoduses that are occurring with increasing
rights of refugees need to be preserved and protecte
time, the responsibility of governments needs to

52

more clearly
populations
conditions o
This is e
ties that all
in absorbin
within a ge
cal popula
just as gre
successful
hardship
Discussic
the need
It sh
in most
States.
made i
numbe
and ot
been a
UN F
terna
I
next
thei
time
to n
suc
tha
te

m
n
v
t

[1]Statement by Edward J. Derwinski, Counselor of the U.S. Department of State,
diciary Committee, September 26, 1983. *Department of State Bulletin.* 83:59–63. D. '83.
*Department of State Bulletin* of December 1983.

creased productivity in the industry and lowered prices. And Philip L. Martin of the University of California at Davis contends that the use of aliens in agriculture is holding back important mechanization.

To some extent, however, the substitution of cheap labor for capital will also be moderated by an expanding economy. Michael L. Wachter of the University of Pennsylvania notes that low-skilled workers may be substitutes for capital, but the increased output they produce also spurs capital investment.

### Welfare Worries

Even those who recognize that the economic benefits of illegal immigrants outweigh the negatives worry that legalizing their status could be costly. They fear that illegals who currently are afraid to seek welfare and jobless benefits will demand them once they gain amnesty, as the Simpson-Mazzoli bill provides. The Office of Management & Budget estimates that welfare costs could go up as much as $10 billion over a three-year period. Concern over this steep increase helps explain the Reagan Administration's failure to endorse the bill.

But this problem, too, may be less severe than OMB expects. It appears that illegals already use welfare programs to a greater degree than previously thought. David Heer of the University of Southern California compared families of workers in Los Angeles County. He found that about the same percentage of families of illegal Mexican workers obtained food stamps and aid to dependent children as did families of Mexican legal immigrants and American citizens of Mexican descent.

Similarly, David S. North of the New TransCentury Foundation in Washington, D.C., found that aliens do receive unemployment benefits. Of 147 illegals arrested by federal authorities in 1975 who re-entered the labor force, 35% received unemployment benefits at some time over the next five years.

Thus, if illegal immigrants are legalized, the number demanding more social services could be far less than expected. In general, fears that a tide of immigrant aliens will wreak economic havoc seem overstated.

## III. "WRETCHED REFUSE"

## EDITOR'S INTRODUCTION

The line dividing refugee from immigrant is often a fine one. Refugees are those fleeing temporary danger or oppression who intend to return once the danger is past. But, once in their host countries, many refugees never return, and therefore become immigrants. This is especially true of refugees who may have a moral claim on the nation of sanctuary. The 600,000 Vietnamese refugees who permanently entered the United States after the fall of Saigon are a case in point, as, to a lesser extent, are the Mariel boat people deported by Cuba in 1980. As refugees are given special consideration in world law and in national immigration policies, the decision about who is a legitimate refugee and who is an immigrant can pose ethical and political problems for the host country. Are Haitians who apply for entry into the United States economic and political refugees escaping an oppressive rightist regime, and thus worthy of a humanitarian welcome (as they themselves claim), or are they simply trying to avoid unpleasant but bearable conditions under a government firmly allied to the United States, and thus not definable as refugees (as U.S. officials currently maintain)? The plight of those Haitians who managed to enter the country (most were held for long periods in squalid detention camps) has been an international embarrassment to the United States.

In this section's first article, Edward J. Derwinski, a senior State Department official, details the global refugee situation as defined by the United States and explains U.S. entry quotas for the major regions affected. Derwinski's description of current policy as "generous and humane" is questioned by Frank Moan in the second selection; Moan, director of the Office of Jesuit Refugee Services, suggests that the quota system is discriminatory and that the United States sets limits for refugee admission that it never intends to fulfill. Gerda Bikales, a member of the Federation for American Immigration Reform (FAIR), argues in an article from the *Humanist* that new ethical guidelines are needed to clarify refugee policy. In her view, a "golden rule" of self-preservation is needed to protect the United States from a deluge of immigrants and refugees.

---

## PROPOSED REFUGEE ADMISSIONS FOR FY 1984[1]

---

Few subjects are of greater human concern in our foreign policy than the plight of the world's refugees. Each decade in the past half century has its record of refugees seeking escape from oppression. In this decade alone we have witnessed three mass flights on a historic scale: 1.6 million refugees from Indochina; 1 million from Ethiopia; and over 3 million from Afghanistan. The human costs of such exoduses can be measured in the loss of people to the home country, often including the ablest and most spirited; the burden of added population to the receiving countries, whether near or far, and the human toll on the refugees themselves.

As in the past, the countries from which the largest numbers of refugees have fled are those that have fallen to communist domination or leadership, for it is in those countries that the basic aspirations of life—which we sum up in the term human rights—are most persistently violated.

As we look to the future there is growing recognition of the need for a full international process of burden sharing to aid refugees. Such a process needs to look for new ways to expand the circle of countries prepared to assist in caring for refugees. We also need to consider what can be done to anticipate and prevent refugee flows, in particular to reduce the size and duration of the massive exoduses that are occurring with increasing frequency. The rights of refugees need to be preserved and protected. At the same time, the responsibility of governments needs to be spelled out

[1]Statement by Edward J. Derwinski, Counselor of the U.S. Department of State, before the Senate Judiciary Committee, September 26, 1983. *Department of State Bulletin.* 83:59–63. D. '83. Reprinted from the *Department of State Bulletin* of December 1983.

more clearly to reduce or eliminate the situations in which entire populations are forced to look to other countries for the minimum conditions of decent life.

This is especially evident as we recognize the growing difficulties that all refugee-receiving countries, including our own, face in absorbing refugees. Even where refugee movements take place within a geographic region they can have severe impact on the local populations and on economic development. The impact can be just as great if refugees are moved to distant third countries. The successful adaptation of some refugees should not obscure the hardship that the refugee experience imposes on all concerned. Discussion of refugee problems must start with a recognition of the need to come to grips with the root causes.

It should be stressed that America's leadership role does not, in most cases, require that refugees be admitted to the United States. A considered approach to refugee programs worldwide has made it possible in the past 2 years to reduce substantially the numbers of refugees for whom resettlement in the United States and other third countries is the appropriate solution. This has been a major U.S. policy objective, one that is supported by the UN High Commissioner for Refugees (UNHCR) and by the international community as a whole.

If prevention is the best cure for a refugee problem, then the next best, clearly, is for refugees to be enabled to return freely to their homelands. Often this cannot take place right away, but in time the factors that caused refugees to flee may change enough to make possible such voluntary repatriation. We have supported such efforts wherever proposed by the UNHCR, always insisting that there be safeguards to assure that the refugees' rights are protected.

Even if voluntary repatriation is not immediately in sight, it makes sense to care for refugees within their region. In many cases neighboring countries have ties of language or ethnic character which ease the acceptance of refugees and facilitate their longer term integration. Such local resettlement also preserves the possibility of the refugees returning eventually to their homelands as conditions change. In general, the expectation needs to be challenged that becoming a refugee equates to distant emigration. Except where required by special circumstances, solutions to refugee situations should be sought close to home.

## International Relief Efforts

Each year since 1981 a growing share of State Department funds allocated to refugee programs aids refugees overseas, with a declining portion devoted to the U.S. admissions program. Wherever possible, and in consultation with the host government and the UNHCR, our contributions support programs aimed at easing the transition to refugee self-sufficiency and long-term solutions. We look to the UNHCR to take the lead in organizing the international aid effort in such a way as to engage the widest possible number of donors and to bring to bear the resources of the appropriate international agencies—the World Food Program, UN Children's Fund (UNICEF), the World Health Organization, and the UN Development Program. Non-UN bodies such as the International Committee of the Red Cross (ICRC) and the League of Red Cross Societies, as well as private humanitarian organizations, also play vital roles in refugee assistance programs. Through these organizations, as well as directly, the United States aids refugees in every part of the world. Our refugee assistance will amount to some $300 million in FY 1983, including Food for Peace commodities, and is likely to come close to that total in FY 1984.

Some of the major assistance programs that we support include:

**Africa.** The countries of Africa have been generous in granting refuge to large numbers of refugees, in many cases providing land for resettlement and conferring citizenship or other legal status on refugees. For our part, the United States has allocated a large proportion of our refugee assistance programs to Africa. In the Horn of Africa, several American private voluntary agencies serve as key operating arms for the UNHCR. The United States supports a number of special projects in such fields as education and health for African refugees and is a leading contributor to the ICRC program which aids refugees in areas of armed conflict and civil strife.

**Central America.** The United States has provided one-third of the support for international agency programs (UNHCR, ICRC, World Food Program) which assist Salvadorans, Guatemalans, and Nicaraguans who have taken refuge in Honduras and other countries of the area. Our programs are designed to encourage and maintain the asylum tradition of the Central American countries.

**Pakistan.** The United States has been a major contributor to UNHCR and other international programs to aid the 2.9 million Afghan refugees in Pakistan—the largest single refugee group in the world. The Government of Pakistan has carried the principal responsibility for assuring basic life support for the refugees within its borders. Some 17 voluntary agencies aid in providing refugee relief and services.

**Palestinians in the Near East.** The United States continues to provide financial support to the UN Relief and Works Agency (UNRWA) which is responsible for assisting Palestine refugees in the Near East. In addition, the United States contributed over $100 million in relief and reconstruction aid for Lebanese and Palestinian displaced persons following the 1982 invasion of Lebanon.

**Thailand and Kampuchea.** The UN border relief operation continues to coordinate relief programs on the Thai-Kampuchean border. Attacks on border camps by Vietnamese military forces from within Kampuchea forced many Khmer to seek temporary refuge further inside Thailand, and the requirements for food and medical aid on the border remain substantial. We are a major contributor to the international antipiracy program organized by UNHCR to assist the governments of the area in protecting refugees from pirate attacks at sea and plan to use the added resources provided by the Congress for an expanded multilateral program.

## International Resettlement Cooperation

Despite the emphasis given to aiding refugees in the regions of their homeland, there continue to be circumstances in which there is no humane alternative to moving refugees to other countries, including the United States. This is particularly so when refugees cannot be cared for in first-asylum countries and there is no prospect for return to the homeland without fear of persecution. In such situations the United States must continue to do its fair share, while recognizing that the responsibility for refugee resettlement is one which properly falls on the entire international community.

In the past year there have been continued actions to broaden the base of refugee resettlement. The UNHCR and the Intergovernmental Committee for Migration (ICM) have each acted within the terms of their mandates to encourage additional nations to admit refugees and to persuade traditional asylum countries to maintain or expand their programs. Significant numbers of refugees—Indochinese and others—are currently accepted by Australia, Canada, the Federal Republic of Germany, and France. Some countries with smaller programs accept handicapped refugees and those needing long-term medical care. Several governments have given commitments to receive refugees rescued at sea. In August of this year the United States met in Honolulu with senior immigration officials of Australia, Canada, and Japan to coordinate programs for Indochinese refugees. We plan to continue such consultations on an expanded basis in the year ahead.

## Proposed Admissions Levels

The admissions ceilings proposed by the President for the coming year reflect these considerations and priorities and are based on a thorough review of U.S. foreign policy interests and humanitarian concerns balanced against the constraints of domestic impact. The numbers recommended for FY 1984 are as follows:

| | |
|---|---|
| Africa | 3,000 |
| East Asia | 50,000 |
| Eastern Europe and the Soviet Union | 12,000 |
| Latin America and the Caribbean | 1,000 |
| Near East and South Asia | 6,000 |
| TOTAL | 72,000 |

Refugee admissions to the United States since enactment of the Refugee Act of 1980 have been as follows:

FY 1981-159,252
FY 1982-97,355
FY 1983-61,000

In each of these years actual admissions have been well below the ceilings set by the President following the consultations with Congress. In the current year the estimated admissions will run some 29,000 below the agreed ceiling of 90,000. It has been our policy to accept only refugees of special concern to the United States, who meet our admissions criteria and are not otherwise excludable, for whom there are no other reasonable resettlement possibilities, and whose admission responds to compelling U.S. foreign policy interests or humanitarian concerns.

**Africa.** Although the great majority of African refugees are cared for within the region, there continue to be individual cases and groups of refugees for whom international resettlement is required. The proposed admissions ceiling of 3,000 will enable us to do our fair share to relieve the pressure in certain areas and to aid refugees who can be cared for in the region only with difficulty. This includes limited numbers of urban refugees who cannot be assimilated readily into rural areas and former political prisoners and other refugees needing resettlement abroad for political or security reasons. Our admissions priorities are responsive to the special claims of refugees with relatives or other ties to the United States, foreign links which themselves sometimes make it more difficult for a refugee to be resettled locally.

**East Asia.** Although the number of new refugees arriving in first-asylum countries of Southeast Asia is down from the peaks of past years, there continue to be some 192,000 currently in first-asylum refugee camps. (This figure does not include an additional 210,000 Khmer in border encampments along the Thai-Kampuchean frontier.) Deep ethnic and national differences and antipathies make resettlement in nearby countries always difficult and in most cases impossible. Consequently, the countries offering temporary refuge—our close friends and allies—remain under heavy domestic political pressure to limit the numbers of refugees in their territory. The proposed admissions ceiling of 50,000 thus responds to urgent foreign policy and strategic factors, as well as considerations of compelling humanitarian concern.

The countries of the Association of South East Asian Nations (ASEAN) have been on the front lines of this refugee emergency since its beginning. For them it represents the direct, visible consequence of oppressive, aggressive policies by the Vietnamese authorities toward their own people and toward the neighboring states of Kampuchea and Laos. For domestic as well as strategic reasons the ASEAN countries have a vital interest in limiting the impact of the refugee influx, and they share our objective of bringing this program to a humane conclusion.

The recent discussions in Honolulu confirmed that this goal is in accord with the policies of the other major resettlement countries aiding Indochinese refugees and with the internationally mandated objectives of the UNHCR. We hope that the downward trend of new arrivals and the combined effort of the countries of the area, the resettlement countries, and the UNHCR will result in a continued reduction of the refugee population which will make it possible to look to the next 2 years as the final stage of this historic program.

Responding to a recent presidential directive, the State and Justice Departments have reached agreement on revised guidelines for refugee processing which spell out in detail the characteristics and categories of various groups with an apparent claim to refugee status. Immigration and Naturalization Service (INS) officers will continue to be responsible for making individual case-by-case determinations for U.S. admissions, but the detailed information in the guidelines should make it possible to evaluate refugee claims on a more consistent basis.

In the current year the total number of Indochinese refugees entering the United States before September 30 is estimated at 39,500, some 24,500 less than the 64,000 ceiling for FY 1983. Another 15,000 Indochinese approved by INS during this year will be in ESL/CO [English-as-a-second-language and cultural orientation] classes or en route to such classes as of the end of this year and will enter the United States under the FY 1984 ceiling.

The proposed East Asia ceiling for the coming year takes account of three programs directed at situations of particular concern to our country:

*Orderly Departure Program (ODP) from Vietnam:* The ODP was established by agreement between the UNHCR and the Vietnamese authorities following the Geneva boat refugee conference in July 1979 to provide a safe, legal alternative to the appalling risks of refugee flight by sea. There was a significant expansion of this program in 1983, bringing the numbers to a monthly departure rate for the United States of close to 1,000 persons. (About the same number depart for other countries.) There are indications that Vietnamese who may be considering illegal flight are at last regarding the ODP as a viable alternative. A significant portion of the FY 1984 numbers for East Asia will be utilized for ODP cases.

*Amerasian Children from Vietnam:* As the committee knows, we have carried out the objective of the Amerasian legislation in the case of Vietnam through the orderly departure program, utilizing refugee numbers as necessary. Vietnamese-American children are of especially compelling concern to many Americans, and we want to be certain that adequate numbers are available to admit all such cases. The total number of Amerasians admitted thus far, including immediate relatives, is over 1,000 persons. The numbers have increased in recent months, and a growing proportion are admitted as refugees.

*"Re-education Camp" Prisoners:* We have long made clear our special concern for those Vietnamese, many of them associated with our past programs in Vietnam, who have been held as political prisoners in so-called "re-education camps," a euphemism for concentration camps. Many such prisoners have been held since 1975 under conditions of severe privation and hardship. Some have been released for "re-education in place," allowed to return to their homes but still deprived of their civil and political rights. We have asked the UNHCR and the ICRC to intervene on behalf of these prisoners, to seek improvement in their conditions of detention, and to attempt to arrange for their release. There can be no question of our obligation to consider such former detainees for admission under our programs. Many, probably most, are likely to qualify under our highest priorities.

Responding to recommendations of this committee, we have strengthened and extended the English-as-a-second-language and cultural orientation programs in the Refugee Processing Centers (RPCs), with close to 90% of working-age Indochinese refugees now receiving this training before they enter the United States, many of them for a full 6 months. Preliminary results of independent studies confirm the value of such overseas language and cultural studies in preparing refugees for entry to the United States. We have also initiated language-training programs for Ethiopian refugees entering the United States from Africa.

In cooperation with the Center for Disease Control of the U.S. Public Health Service, we have taken a series of actions to improve the medical screening and treatment of refugees before their departure for the United States, with strengthened followup measures, where needed, by public health officials in the United States. Improved medical facilities are planned for the RPCs to be provided in part through contributions from the Japanese Government and private sources. In addition to the improvement in health care for refugees that this will make possible, it is clear that the costs of treating medical problems abroad are significantly below the costs of comparable treatment in the United States.

**Soviet Union and Eastern Europe.** The past year has been marked by a continued decline in the number of refugees permitted to leave the Soviet Union and continued substantial but relatively stable numbers of Poles and other East Europeans in temporary refuge in Western Europe. The total number of Jewish refugees coming to the United States from the Soviet Union fell below 1,000 this year for the first time since Jewish emigration began to be permitted in the early 1970s. The decline has been accompanied by public campaigns in the USSR alleging that all Soviet Jews wishing to depart have done so, a claim rejected by concerned experts in our own country and Israel. The number of Armenians coming to the United States from the U.S.S.R. has continued at the 300–400 level of last year, also a historic low since this program began.

The majority of the refugee numbers for this region, accordingly, are being utilized for Poles and other East Europeans. Most such refugees manage to make their way to Austria, the Federal Republic of Germany, and other West European nations where they are able to apply for permanent resettlement elsewhere. The largest single group are Poles who were already in Western Europe when martial law was declared in their country at the end of 1981. There are few signs of Poles returning home following the announced "suspension" of martial law in July 1983, and many Poles outside their country continue to seek opportunities for permanent refuge in the West.

In the past year, some 500 former political detainees in Poland, mostly Solidarity activists who have been released from prison, were permitted to travel to the United States with their families. The former prisoners make initial application at American posts in Poland and are assisted in further processing and travel to the United States by the Intergovernmental Committee for Migration (ICM). A comparable number of ex-detainees have been accepted by other countries.

There continues to be a substantial flow of refugees from other East European countries, many of whom can be expected to come to the United States. Since the Second World War, East European refugees have looked to our country as a safe haven from the communist regimes of their homelands. Many continue to do so.

**Latin America and the Caribbean.** Although there are substantial numbers of refugees and persons displaced by fighting and civil strife in Central America, the tradition of asylum in neighboring countries remains well established. Our programs are designed to encourage and support that tradition. The proposed ceiling of 1,000 will enable us to relieve situations of special concern by admitting to the United States former and current political prisoners, immediate relatives of refugees already in the United States, and persons with especially compelling needs. Our admissions will include a limited number of Salvadorans among those granted amnesty by the Government of El Salvador and their families, up to 200 persons in all. We continue to provide major support to UNHCR and other international assistance programs throughout the region.

**Near East and South Asia.** The proposed admissions ceiling of 6,000 will make it possible to admit selected cases out of the many refugees who have received temporary refuge within this area. By far the largest number are Afghans who have left their country since the Soviet invasion in late 1979: some 2.9 million now in Pakistan, a sizable number in Iran, and smaller totals in other countries including the United States—in total well over 3 million. The great majority are tribal people who look forward to the possibility of returning to Afghanistan and for whom temporary resettlement is the preferred solution. As is the case in other regions, the primary U.S. response has been a major commitment to supporting the international relief programs established to care for the refugees within the area. In Pakistan these programs include self-sufficiency projects aimed at enabling refugees to contribute to their own support in their situations of temporary exile. The U.S. admissions program for Afghans is carried out on an individual basis and applies primarily to those with close family or other ties to the United States.

During the past year we have also implemented an admissions program for Iranians forced to leave their country following the overthrow of the Shah and the rise to power of the Ayatollah Khomeini. Based on our experience in 1983, we are extending our admissions program in 1984 to Iranian refugees outside their country, but not permanently settled, even if they do not have relatives or other ties to the United States. There has been special concern about such groups as the Bahais, Christians, Jews, and others singled out for discrimination by the current regime. Our admissions program will continue to offer a safe alternative for these and other victims of oppression.

### Domestic Considerations

As reported to the committee in the mid-year consultations and in our testimony on the reauthorization of the Refugee Act of 1980, we have taken a series of actions aimed at improving the integration of refugees into our communities and cities. We are mindful that in bringing refugees to the United States we are, in effect, admitting future new Americans. Our goal has been a program that assures that all refugees coming to our country are given a positive start on the path to self-support through employment as productive members of our society. The history of our programs shows this has been the case in the past, with many of yesterday's refugees and their children becoming leaders in our society today. We want to be sure our programs continue to serve that objective.

We have continued our expanded program of working with the private voluntary agencies to assure that refugees receive the full range of assistance specified in our cooperative agreements. The voluntary agencies have a long record of helping refugees, in this country and abroad, for which they merit full recognition. At the same time, we believe that they and we have benefited from the monitoring of their operations that is now in effect on a continuing basis. There have been management reforms to establish self-monitoring by voluntary agencies, to strengthen contacts between local affiliates and welfare offices, to insure a minimum of 90 days' active assistance to each refugee, and to provide special attention to children who may be vulnerable to placement breakdowns, all serving the overall goal of assisting the refugees and their families in moving toward productive self-sufficiency.

In cooperation with the Department of Health and Human Services, we are taking advantage of the lower rate of refugee arrivals in 1983 and 1984 to bring about constructive changes in a program that grew rapidly in previous years, to some extent stretching the capabilities of all concerned. There is now in place a network of national, state, local, governmental, and private cooperation capable of assisting refugees already here and meeting the needs of the future. We believe the reception and placement program is working well and that further improvement can be expected in line with recommendations of the refugee assistance amendments of 1982 and the revised provisions of the cooperative agreements that have been presented to this committee.

## Conclusion

Our refugee programs are an essential part of our foreign policy and continue a generous and humane American tradition. The admissions proposals outlined above will enable us to continue to do our fair share while helping to sustain the far greater numbers of refugees being assisted overseas. We hope they will have your support.

---

## THE REFUGEE PROBLEM: A LOOK AT THE NUMBERS[2]

---

There are lies, damn lies and statistics. But statistics do begin to give a picture. What picture do they begin to draw of the refugee situation?

Counted refugees number 7,816,200 in 60 countries. Not so bad, if they were evenly divided. Each country would have only 130,270. But of those 7,816,200, Pakistan has 2,800,000 whereas Nigeria has only 400. In fact, those countries grouped as being in the Middle East/South Asia area account for 5,295,600 or 67 percent of all counted refugees. This is due principally to the 3,304,000 Afghans who have abandoned their homeland since the Soviet takeover. Present indications are that few of these five million will ever be settled in a third country. How the countries of refuge will continue to handle such a massive problem is far from clear.

While there are still over seven million counted refugees, another 2,765,700 have been settled in foreign countries. Of these, 1,003,000 (the largest number accepted by any single country) have found legal adoption in the United States. The United States is also the largest financial contributor to international refugee aid agencies, spending, in FY82 alone, $244.4 million. Tempted as we may be to pride ourselves on these two achievements, we should temper our elation with the balancing factors. Yes, the United States gives the most money, but it stands only eighth among countries on the basis of contributions per citizen. The Scandinavian countries of Norway, Denmark and Sweden lead the list. Norway surpasses us by donating more than three times as much per citi-

---

[2]Reprint of a magazine article by Frank Moan, S.J., director of the Office of Jesuit Refugee Services, Washington, D.C. *America* 150:208–9. Mr. 24, '84. Reprinted with permission of America Press, Inc., 106 West 56th Street, New York, NY 10019. Copyright © 1984. All rights reserved.

zen; Denmark and Sweden are close to that mark. Norway do-
nates $3.83 per citizen while the United States contributes $1.05
per citizen. Canada is also ahead of us, giving $1.14 per citizen.
Nor can the United States boast of being first among countries of
resettlement as far as the ratio of refugees to a country's population is concerned. There we rank third. Australia has accepted one
refugee for every 47 of its citizens; Canada one for every 69; the
United States is next, after a wide gap, admitting one refugee for
every 231 of its citizens.

Also of note is the fact that this country has never admitted the
numbers of refugees that it has, itself, provided for in recent years.
While our official ceiling in FY81 was to admit 217,000, we admitted only 159,300. In FY82 we officially provided for accepting
140,000; we accepted 97,300. In FY83 we officially welcomed 90,
000; in fact, we welcomed only 61,681. For FY84 President Reagan has set a ceiling of 72,000; Attorney General William French
Smith has publicly declared that that number will not be reached,
despite the fact that nearly eight million counted refugees are in
need.

Take one step further. If one looks, for example, at the 90,000
provided for in FY83, the pattern of actual admission is even more
puzzling. In actual numbers the largest group to come were from
Southeast Asia, 39,408 out of a possible 64,000. So we admitted
62 percent of that quota. But the highest percentage, 91 percent,
came from the Near East/South Asia area, 5,465 arriving out of
a possible and mere 6,000, where more than five million refugees
are located. Next, with 89 percent, were those from the Soviet
Union and Eastern Europe, 13,492 out of a possible 15,000
places. Right behind, with 88 percent, were those admitted from
Africa, 2,648 out of a quota of 3,000 for a continent housing two
million counted refugees. At the very bottom of the ladder come
refugees from Latin America and the Caribbean. From that whole
area we made provision for only 2,000, and we actually accepted
only 668, or 33 percent.

Questions spontaneously arise. Why, for example, is 89 percent of the quota from Eastern Europe, where there are less than
0.4 percent of the world's refugees, filled while only 33 percent
of the quota from Latin America and the Caribbean is admitted?

And on the basis of what criteria have the President's advisers suggested to him the allotments he has ordered for FY84, namely, 3,000 Africans and 1,000 Latin Americans and Caribbeans? This represents no variation in the figure for Africa from FY83, but a 50 percent decrease in the number to be admitted from Latin America and the Caribbean. This is so despite the President's directive to his Coordinator for Refugee Affairs, which singles out for admission those "persons in Vietnam with past or present ties to the U.S." as well as "political prisoners and persons in imminent danger of loss of life and their family members, in countries of Latin America and the Caribbean." Is there reason for being optimistic that in FY84 the situation in that area will so improve that we can cut our meager ceiling by 50 percent? With such allocations as have been ordered for FY84, will the percentages of actual admission be comparable to FY83? If so, on what basis?

Every nation would like the refugee problem to go away. Indications are that, quite the contrary, the problem will grow in the years ahead. The United States, among other nations, has to examine its own posture toward refugees, especially if, as one study suggests, the superpowers (of which the United States is one) are responsible for the refugee crisis. It seems strangely inconsistent that a nation of refugees cannot develop a stance consistent with its own historical experience. Nor should that stance be founded on "notions of communal guilt and good samaritanism," as a special consultant to the Office of the U.S. Coordinator for Refugee Affairs has implied we have done in the past. If a nation of refugees forgets its past, how can it plan its future?

## A NEW IMMIGRATION ETHIC FOR THE U.S.: UPDATING THE GOLDEN RULE FOR THE GLOBAL VILLAGE[3]

Since 1975 the United States has resettled some 600,000 refugees from Indochina. Yet, the holding camps in Thailand and in other countries of first asylum are full of people awaiting entry into the United States and would surely be more crowded still if word were not circulating that resettlement in the United States is becoming more difficult.

During that same period, the United States accepted some 350,000 refugees from Cuba, Haiti, Central America, and Eastern Europe, as well as many millions of immigrants, both legal and illegal.

Many more millions are hoping to rebuild their lives in the United States, even as the American people are becoming increasingly apprehensive about the social and economic costs of such open-ended admission policies and are demanding greater restrictions.

Behind the creation of a very sizable Vietnamese-American community within a very short period of time lie several factors of far-reaching consequence.

First, one would have to mention the tremendous population explosion in all parts of the less developed world. Overpopulation itself is an actual or potential cause of instability; furthermore, every upheaval displaces larger numbers of persons than would be the case if the area were less populated. Thus, refugee buildups are very rapid, and the sheer number of unfortunate people in flight commands world attention.

Another critical new development is the instant electronic communications technology which can quickly bring the suffering of the most remote and unfamiliar people, from every corner of the world, right into our living room.

[3]Reprint of a magazine article by Gerda Bikales, assistant director of the Federation for American Immigration Reform (FAIR). This article first appeared in *The Humanist,* issue of March/April 1983 (43:12+), and is reprinted by permission.

Finally, we have the means of physically removing thousands of people from the locus of their misery by bringing them to the United States. Only a few short hours in the air separate the most backward Laotian peasant from the country he so hopes to make his own.

These innovations, unknown to earlier generations, are playing havoc with the traditional guidelines we call upon in trying to meet our moral obligations toward the world's less fortunate human beings.

The most fundamental principle voiced by society's seats of moral authority is invariably some version of the Golden Rule: Love thy neighbor as thyself. The rule is deeply ingrained in individuals raised in Judeo-Christian cultures. It underlies our standard codes of neighborliness. Appeals to it can produce collective acts of generosity on a very large scale, as the presence of 600,000 Indochinese residents in the United States amply demonstrates. It can perhaps be said that the internalization of the Golden Rule is considered the true hallmark of civilized human beings.

It should be mentioned, though this is not emphasized in theological thought, that there is a practical aspect to the Golden Rule that strongly reinforces its moral dictum. "Do unto others as you would have them do unto you" is also a sensible *quid pro quo* that tacitly implies: be helpful to your neighbor in his time of need, so that you may count on him to reciprocate when you need assistance. The compelling force of the Golden Rule lies precisely in that its lofty appeal to conscience is reinforced by the practical wisdom of the command.

With the advent of instant electronic communications, the neighborhood has been expanded well beyond the confines of one's community to include the whole world. The suffering of a dispossessed family in El Salvador can be made every bit as vivid as that of the folks next door. More so, perhaps. On our television screens we can watch their desperation presented in an emotional tone that our next door neighbors would be too embarrassed to use.

This technological revolution poses a new challenge to the Golden Rule: How do I love my neighbor as myself, when *every* poor and downtrodden human being in this overpopulated world *is* my neighbor?

*The Search for Guidelines*

The above question is very new. Moral decision making in the past tended to be based on absolute principles and disregarded considerations of scale entirely.

But, resources being finite, how many of the world's millions of unfortunate people is one to help? Is it better to share more fully with a few individuals or is less help to more people the better choice?

We have few guidelines as we earnestly grope for answers.

Traditionalist authorities might want to call upon the life of St. Francis of Assisi to support their interpretation of moral obligation. This revered saint has given us an inspiring example of a man born to wealth who chooses to abandon its comforts and to live a life of shared poverty as a mendicant among lepers and outcasts. But renunciation is not a serviceable model for us. The call to our conscience is not for us to share the misery of the most miserable among us but for help to improve their lives through our acts of compassion and generosity. The number of totally selfless saints a modern society can afford is rather small. A nation of good-hearted mendicants cannot long sustain itself, let alone help numerous others.

The wise sharing of our possessions, rather than their renunciation, is a model that is wanted. Here we have the example of St. Martin de Tours, who gave away one-half of his cloak to a naked beggar. One wonders, however, what St. Martin would have done had he encountered twenty naked and shivering beggars on his path. Would he have selected one or two for covering and allowed the others to freeze? If so, on what basis would these fortunate few have been selected over all the other unfortunates? Or would the saint have split his garment into twenty-one equal but inadequate pieces, which would have really shielded no one from the cold? Are both decisions equally virtuous, though the latter is patently foolish?

## The Quantitative Aspects of Charity

For lack of better quantitative guidelines for charitable behavior, we can perhaps draw upon the universally recognized prescription of tithing. The concept that men and women of conscience should spend a tenth of their revenues on the Church and on good works has long been well known throughout the Judeo-Christian world. It is probably to be interpreted as a minimum for each of us, to be exceeded by those who can afford more. A source often quoted in the Jewish literature on *Tsedakah* proposes a maximum contribution of one-fifth of one's revenues, and cautions that those who give more run the risk of becoming paupers themselves.

But this is hardly a mainstream Jewish position on charity. A more meaningful inhibition on excessive giving could be deduced from strong prohibitions in Jewish law against suicide. To knowingly risk serious injury to oneself and one's family, albeit in the cause of helping another, could be considered suicidal behavior, which is abhorrent.

In modern societies, the functions served by tithing with the Church have been largely taken over by governments. Through taxation, Americans already contribute far more than the traditional one-tenth to numerous social programs designed to help the sick, the elderly, the handicapped, the very young, and the poor among us. Through taxation, they also contribute to numerous aid programs abroad, including significant payments to the United Nations High Commission for Refugees, to alleviate the suffering of millions of uprooted refugees.

In addition to "charity through taxation," Americans give readily to numerous private good works, both here and in other countries. Whenever and whatever disaster strikes, Americans can be counted on for generous assistance. Thus, through private and public channels, Americans are fulfilling the moral obligation of tithing.

## *Religious Authority in a Secular Society*

America, founded by deeply devout people seeking the freedom to exercise their stern religious precepts, is nevertheless a determinedly secular society. Religion has surely been the premiere spiritual influence in our common culture—but by no means the only one. Preoccupation with things spiritual is not an especially typical national characteristic. Unfriendly critics may call us materialistic, but that really misses the point. More positively, it can be said that we are rationalists and pragmatists and that we pride ourselves on our good common sense. Science, and the technological changes it has spawned, have markedly shaped us and influenced the character of our people and our country.

In interpreting what sort of immigration and refugee policies would be in compliance with the Judeo-Christian Golden Rule, the conclusions reached by the religious leadership tend to differ greatly from those reached by the vast majority of the American public. The root of the difference lies in the classic dichotomy between faith and reason.

At issue is the question of how real, how immediate, and how tyrannical are our resource constraints. Men of unshakable faith can afford to be rather less concerned about all this, in the firm belief that "God will provide." Resource management is definitely much simpler for those who accept the verity of the parable of the Seven Loaves of Bread and a Few Little Fish.

Most Americans, however, whether church-affiliated or not, will tend to rely on their empirical observations that quantities do matter. In a world of limits, they sense that these somehow apply to giving and that we are in danger of stretching these limits too far in our refugee admissions policies.

We see today that these divergent understandings of the nature of resource constraints have produced a vocal coalition of religious figures who use their influence with the political leadership to plead for more refugee (as well as immigrant) admissions; on the other side we see much of the American public, badgered by job shortages, budget deficits, an uncertain energy future, and suffering from what has been called "compassion fatigue," now openly resisting more admissions.

Democratic societies can accommodate many divergent viewpoints, of course. It would hardly create a ripple of interest if those still anchored to the moral standards of a time when neighbor meant the people next door would follow their own conscience and share all their personal possessions with the world's suffering poor. But refugee admissions to the United States are not the religious leadership's to give. By law, that gift must come from the American people, many of whom now perceive a clear need to cut back on refugee entries.

In our society, religious institutions and their leaders are highly respected and exert great moral influence; they have, however, been carefully kept from exercising official authority. The perception is thus created that their moral influence gets skillfully translated into political coercion for a more charitable posture through a process somewhat akin to moral blackmail. The technique has been highly successful, but it inevitably creates resentment.

The flaw in the attitude displayed by the religious leadership is the fact that, once the refugees have been brought to the United States, the costs of their resettlement do not fall crushingly upon the religious institutions but are imposed upon the American commonwealth. A pattern of resettlement practice has developed that concentrates the prestige and the moral glory of the resettlement effort in the hands of the religious humanitarians but leaves the taxpayer picking up the tab.

This *modus operandi*—the resettlement of refugees by church-sponsored agencies with public money—has attracted a goodly number of secular humanitarians to the fold. Catholic Charities, Lutheran Social Services, the Hebrew Immigrant Aid Society are among the dominant forces in the field. The Tolstoi Foundation and Czechoslovak Relief have also found roles. And so has that entire spectrum known as the helping professions and human services specialists, for whom the continued refugee influx represents not only a livelihood but, indeed, a *raison d'etre* and a source of social prestige.

Together, the religious, secular, and professional humanitarians form an influential lobby that works effectively for continued large-scale refugee and immigrant admissions, despite growing opposition at the grass-roots level to these policies.

## The Permanent Crisis

The coalition of religious and secular humanitarian special interests has been very successful in stretching the definition of refugee and in securing from the political leadership continued large-scale refugee admissions into the United States. However, it has not had much success in changing the increasingly negative attitudes of many Americans toward this influx.

By any available measurement—national public opinion polls, constituent mail to congressional offices, offers from volunteers to sponsor incoming refugees—there has been a steady decline of support for more refugee settlement in the United States.

One can cite many obvious reasons for this development, including the deteriorating state of our economy. Let us consider some of the less obvious ones:

1. *The Failure of Guilt.* In view of their historic generosity toward the world's poor and homeless, Americans fail to feel wicked because they are not doing more; on the contrary, they tend to perceive the pressure from the humanitarian lobby as a case of the self-righteous browbeating the righteous.

2. *The Obligation Toward America's Disadvantaged.* A generation ago, Americans pledged themselves to helping our own historically discriminated-against minorities move toward full participation in American life. This has required enormous sacrifices on the part of the majority, not only in unprecedented outlays of money for social programs but also, through affirmative action and other compensatory programs, the sacrificing of opportunities for themselves and their children in the interest of greater social equality. The promise to disadvantaged Americans is still not fulfilled, and in fact many rational persons believe that large-scale refugee and immigrant admissions tend to delay progress in this area by inflating economic competition at the bottom of the ladder.

3. *The Permanent Crisis and Psychological Self-Preservation.* In years past, refugee "crises" seemed to be temporary dilemmas that really could be resolved permanently through swift resettlement in another country, particularly the United States. Under such assumptions, we enacted legislation to accept some 400,000 displaced persons after World War II and again 100,000 Hungar-

ians in 1956. The Cuban exodus that started after Castro came to power brought us some one million refugees over a period of two decades. It should have given us pause to reflect on the chain-effect of this flow, but it occurred at a time of record prosperity, preoccupation with the war in Vietnam, and with civil unrest at home. Its essentially never-ending nature was hardly examined at all.

Beginning with the airlift of some 100,000 Indochinese refugees in the wake of our pull-out from Vietnam, we have seen a steady succession of refugee crises. The first wave of Indochinese refugees were accepted on the basis of their direct association with Americans during the war years, and the assumed dangers these individuals would face in the communist take-over. In subsequent waves, the American connection with those in flight became more tenuous, and the term *refugee* underwent constant reinterpretation. Since the major Indochinese "boat people" crisis of 1979, the flow of Laotians, Cambodians, and Vietnamese over land and sea has continued, though the pace has slowed. In 1980, we saw the Mariel exodus that brought 125,000 Cubans to southern Florida. An unknown but significant number of poor Haitians have been arriving in unseaworthy vessels, claiming political asylum. It is estimated that some 600,000 Salvadorans are now illegally in the United States, many claiming asylum as political refugees. Thousands of Poles are fleeing to Vienna in the hope of resettlement in the United States.

These unceasing crises tend to have a dulling effect over time. This is not mean-spiritedness but a psychological survival mechanism that sets in gradually after emotionally wrenching expenditures of empathy. Extraordinary mobilization of compassion cannot be maintained indefinitely; to stay psychologically and emotionally balanced, we must "turn off" and go on with living our own lives.

4. *The Reciprocity Factor.* It is especially difficult to adhere to the most generous interpretation of the Golden Rule when the "neighbor" is a stranger in a distant land. In the case of refugees from very different cultures in unfamiliar lands, the reciprocity assumption is very weak, and does little to reinforce the charitable act.

Yet Americans, like other people of goodwill, can become deeply aroused again and again when a new military or political catastrophe is visited upon some corner of the world, producing dire distress that is vividly brought home via the electronic media. Their most generous impulses are reawakened, and once again they look to the traditional sources of moral authority for guidance.

The real crisis for the American public is the predictability of the response they can expect from the moral authorities they consult on the question of moral obligation. Invariably, the answers belong to the pre-Global Village era: "Open your door, open your heart, open your pocketbook."

Unfortunately, this is no longer functional advice. The symbolic resettlement of a relatively small number of true political refugees is surely desirable and consistent with the highly developed benevolent affections of our people, but massive refugee settlement in the United States has ceased to be a practical option. In a heavily populated world, the capacity to unleash disasters and to inflict suffering far exceeds this nation's capacity to absorb the victims.

The humanitarian establishment has been notably reticent to re-examine the meaning of neighborliness in the Global Village. It has been unwilling to acknowledge America's limits, and to assuage and comfort the conscience of our people seeking to do what's right.

The attitude of our moral authorities is not likely to change— at least not as long as the government continues to pay for the resettlement work done by churches and other "humanitarian" lobbies, instead of requiring them to carry the costs of resettling the refugees they bring in.

We thus find ourselves in a moral leadership vacuum that must be filled. It is hoped that a new generation of theologians and secular ethicists will soon arise, steeped in the ecology and demography of the Global Village, to lead us in the task of articulating to the people and the political leadership a new Golden Rule for the Global Village.

# IV. POLICY AND REFORM

## EDITOR'S INTRODUCTION

As a nation of immigrants, the United States has always had an immigration policy. The passage of naturalization laws was one of the first acts of Congress. Regulations limiting immigration began to be implemented in the mid-1870s, just prior to the unprecedented immigration levels of 1880–1914, when an average of nearly a million people entered the country each year. Later policy has largely been elaborations and revisions of the various restrictive statutes, from ethnic quotas to laws designed to protect American wage levels, passed during and just after those years. Vestiges of the notorious "national origins" system, a set of racially and ethnically biased immigration quotas instituted in 1921, still remain in the refugee statutes and were not eliminated from the immigration code until 1978, when a single, annual global ceiling on the number of immigrants was established.

The liberalization of immigration laws since the mid-1960s has resulted in immigration levels approaching those of the turn of the century. With recent immigrants becoming so visible a part of American society, immigration policy is again a matter of acute public concern. Organizations such as the Federation for American Immigration Reform (FAIR) agitate for stiff restrictions on immigration, while ethnic groups, fearing the reinstatement of discriminatory quotas, are just as vehement in opposing restrictions.

Recent legislative action on immigration has centered on reforms recommended in 1981 by the Select Commission on Immigration and Refugee Policy. The Simpson-Mazzoli bill, whose controversial proposals for restrictive reform are presented by Senator Simpson in the first selection in this section and debated in the following articles, was passed by the Senate in 1983 and in a slightly different version by the House in mid-1984. Although the bill's immediate future is in question—it faces a possible veto by President Reagan, who will not want to alienate Hispanic voters in an election year—a similar bill may well pass in future.

Despite the general agreement among politicians of all parties that something must be done to control illegal immigration and clarify the status of illegal permanent residents, normal political loyalties have little to do with these issues. Some conservatives agree with some liberals that illegal aliens strain the welfare system, take jobs from Americans, and should therefore be excluded. Other spokesmen for both conservative and liberal points of view argue that aliens do work that Americans refuse and should be admitted as part of a policy of American hospitality. This section surveys the variety of opinions, first presenting the opposed positions of Senators Alan K. Simpson and Edward M. Kennedy.

Next, John Donohue's article lays out the issues in the current discussion. The case for restrictive reform is made at length by Georges Fauriol in the third selection. Next, Geoffrey Rips sharply criticizes Simpson-Mazzoli and U.S. immigration policies in general, noting that indiscriminate foreign adventurism and American industry's need for cheap labor are at the root of the country's immigration problems. In the final essay, Julian Simon pleads for an open-door policy, claiming that immigration, legal or otherwise, invigorates the national economy and spirit.

## SHOULD CONGRESS ADOPT THE PENDING "IMMIGRATION REFORM AND CONTROL ACT"?[1]

### *Pro* *

This is the immigration reform and control act of 1983. It is something I commend to you. I spoke here 8 months ago and presented the case that our present immigration laws no longer serve

[1] From *Congressional Digest.* 62:195–224. Ag./S.' 83 and Senate Report 98–62, Ap. 21, '85.

*From an address to the U.S. Senate, April 28, 1983, by Alan K. Simpson, Senator from Wyoming. Reprinted from *Congressional Digest.* 62:195–224. Ag./S. '83.

the national interest, no longer promote the well-being of the majority of the American people. Eight months ago I reported to you that immigration to the United States was out of control. I reported to you also the first duty of a sovereign nation was to control its borders. We do not.

I regret to inform you that on this date, in spite of many of my colleagues' best efforts, the situation is still so, still true. Not only the American people but people the world over know that the United States cannot perform the very first function of a sovereign nation: We cannot control our own borders.

I continue to feel very deeply that uncontrolled immigration is one of the greatest threats to the future of this country—uncontrolled immigration—to American values, traditions, institutions, and the way in which we live.

In contrast, controlled immigration has been one of the finest traditions and the finest things of our remarkable heritage. We have no desire to change that.

Last August, I informed you that net immigration—that is, legal plus illegal—probably exceeded 750,000 per year. That is still true today.

I told you the asylum backlog had grown from 5,000 to 105,000, and today that backlog is over 143,000.

Further, the INS apprehended nearly 1 million illegal aliens last year. This year the apprehension rate has increased by more than 50 percent. Hundreds of thousands of illegal immigrants still cross our borders each year and some estimate the annual inflow at 500,000 persons. Of course, I think with the latest figures there are many more.

Here are the latest figures: 108,000 human beings were apprehended at our borders last month, in 1 month. We anticipate that we apprehend one out of four. Some say one out of five. Those are the numbers.

You have to talk about numbers because numbers are human beings, but those are the numbers. Illegal immigration continues to depress wages and working conditions for American workers, especially low-income, low-skilled Americans who are the most likely to face direct competition.

Illegal immigrants continue to remain a fearful, exploitable subclass in American society, and I believe that the widespread flouting of our Nation's immigration laws still leads to a disrespect for our laws and our institutions in general.

In short, then, the problems remain. Nothing has changed. In most areas, the immigration problem has only deeply worsened.

But there have been some important changes in the bill since it was last before this body. Those changes have been reasonable and have improved the legislation. They have been acceptable to me. Amendments were adopted in committee to provide even more protection against any possible discriminatory effects of employer sanctions. In addition to the Presidential reports on the possible effects of employer sanctions on minorities, we have added a requirement that is very important: The GAO is to report annually on any discrimination against minorities or any undue burden on U.S. employers caused by the legislation. Both the Judiciary Committees and the Labor Committees of each House of Congress are required to hold hearings on these reports and make recommendations to their respective Houses.

We have also provided an authorization for additional appropriations to the EEOC and the Department of Labor in order to provide additional enforcement of present employment discrimination laws and present wage and hour laws.

We have strengthened the provisions for family reunification by reinstating the "fifth preference"—there was a serious debate on that in the last session—for unmarried brothers and sisters. And we have moved up the filing date to the date of enactment of this legislation.

Finally, we have strengthened the enforcement provisions by providing for funding of the bill at $200 million to carry out the legislation in 1984.

As we continue to demand better enforcement of our Nation's immigration laws, we must support that demand with proper funding. We have not done that in the past.

I recommended this bill to my colleagues 8 months ago. I recommend it to you now. I can say that. It is a better bill than the one that passed here by a vote of 80 to 19 in August 1982. I am pleased with the improvements.

In attempting to propose these reasonable immigration reforms, reforms which I sincerely hope and feel deeply are free of meanness and nativism and xenophobia, it is too bad a word like that is so difficult to communicate. It is such a simple gut reaction. It means fear of foreigners.

Those things are not in this bill or it would not have progressed this far.

I have learned much in the process, but one thing principally is this: This is actually a continuing, running gun battle with tunnel vision, short-term special interests constantly cutting—I think the word actually would be slashing—across the long-term national interest. We must recognize that the American public continues to overwhelmingly support immigration reform. Indeed, all recent polls disclose that more than 90 percent of the citizens of this country feel we must regain control of our borders.

Immigration reform can be a significant test of a more common thesis of U.S. politics. This will be the test: Is U.S. politics increasingly controlled by narrow and wholly selfish special interests rather than being representative of the broad public will? We shall find that out once again.

The entire issue is a very, very tough one. It is a political no-win situation in every sense. It generates feelings and accusations of guilt, fear, emotionalism, and racism, and it is very susceptible to being a vehicle to engage in good old high drama.

The bill we recommend today is a fair, workable, humane approach to controlling illegal and legal immigration. A wide diversity of public interest groups involved in immigration support it— the editorial writers of all the major newspapers and dailies and weeklies throughout the United States; citizens of this country; the administration with its support—there is no partisanship in this issue. There never has been. Its supporters and its detractors come from the full spectrum of philosophies. If we do not act in a timely and a rational manner to control our borders, I am deeply concerned that, in the near future, we shall find that we have come to a debate which is increasingly strident, unpleasant, and clouded by a return to the past in immigration reform, which has always been characterized by racism or restrictionism or nativism.

I do not want to be part of that and other ugly elements which we have successfully excised from this reform effort. We have made a special, special attempt at all points in the debate and the hearings to recognize the deep problems that the Hispanic community has with the legislation. I have said to them in all honesty that it seems to me that the worst thing that could happen to the Hispanic community is to do nothing. Then we shall begin to deal in this body, as we always deal in this body, with emergency, short-term solutions, which will include this trip, then, more money for the INS, more money for the border patrol—after all, we have not done anything, so why not just get them off their backs and give them money to do their work?—more intrusions into the workplace, more sweeps. And, finally, after that, after an employer has been busted five or six times, he or she will come to the recognition of one thing, as all Americans: "I am not going to go through that hassle any more. There is a way to do that for me; I am never going to hire anybody again who 'looks foreign.'"

That would be the truest and most devastating form of discrimination.

I respectfully submit this to my colleagues. I submit it in all sincerity as a work product that came down through the Select Committee—a very diverse group, indeed—through the Ford administration, through the Carter administration, through the Reagan administration. I always say to people—and it is still not too late to say this because we have time for the debate—that if you do not embrace the various provisions of this proposed legislation, please furnish us an alternative. But no fair quoting from the Statue of Liberty, because the moving words of Emma Lazarus on that statue—and that statement is not a smart-aleck statement— because the moving words on that statue in the harbor, on that Lady of the Golden Door, do not say "Send us everybody you've got, legally or illegally."

I commend the legislation to my colleagues for their attention.

### Con *

Although I am concerned over specific provisions of this legislation, I am even more concerned over the larger issue of the migration pressures our country will encounter in the decades ahead. I am concerned this legislation is moving forward in a kind of vacuum, and that we will be deluding ourselves if we think this legislation will really solve the many immigration problems our country—along with many others—faces today. At best this is a band-aid to a potential hemorrhage—a very tentative step in a long-term process.

Every day it becomes clearer that the complex migration problems, which are growing around the world, will require greater international action. Domestic laws and actions alone are no longer sufficient. Economic and developmental problems in neighboring countries—or even in countries far away—will have more impact upon migration to the United States than any combination of domestic laws or policies. And violence and conflict can produce a flow of people that only concerted international action can deal with.

There are no easy answers. But it is imperative that we understand that migration is an international issue, and not merely a domestic concern. It will require far greater international cooperation than we have undertaken to date.

This bill is moving forward without adequate consultations by the Executive Branch with our neighbors. If we are to achieve genuine cooperation we must consult in advance, before changes in our immigration policies are set.

Unilateral policies, like fences, do not always make good neighbors. During our consideration of this bill we must give greater weight to this concern and the Administration must give greater evidence that it, too, is pursuing it.

A fundamental concern I have about this bill is that it must not become a vehicle for discriminatory action against Hispanic Americans and other minority groups. Immigrants and undocumented aliens must not become scapegoats for the serious prob-

*A minority view by Massachusetts Senator Edward M. Kennedy in Senate Report 98–62, dated April 21, 1983. Reprinted in *Congressional Digest* 62:195–224. Ag./S. '83.

lems our country faces today. In too many quarters, migrants and undocumented aliens are being unfairly blamed for the current high levels of unemployment in the United States.

We must be extremely cautious to avoid legislative action that raises the level of intolerance and discrimination in our society. The employer sanctions provisions present this danger, and I regret that the Committee did not accept an amendment that addresses this issue.

I have in the past supported legal sanctions against employers who knowingly hire undocumented aliens. I have done so as a matter of principle; it is wrong that the sanctions under current law fall solely on the undocumented aliens, not on employers who may be exploiting them. The government needs stronger enforcement tools to deal with the serious problem of employers who engage in a pattern and practice of hiring and exploiting undocumented aliens.

It is frequently heard today that immigration to the United States is, somehow, bad—that the numbers are too high, the impact is undesirable, and the consequences for the future are negative. These implications fly in the face of American history, and I reject them, as did the Select Commission on Immigration and Refugee Policy.

Illegal immigration must be controlled. But there is no evidence that the current levels of *legal* immigration are dangerous or contrary to our national interests.

The Commission rejected the notion that current immigration is destabilizing or somehow threatening to our national unity. Although the admission of immigrants and refugees to the United States has increased numerically over the past decade, the proportion of foreign born citizens in the United States is dramatically lower than at any previous point in our history. In 1890, the percentage of foreign born was 14.7; in 1970, it was down to a bare 4.7.

Veiled reference is also frequently made to the more than 800,000 immigrants and refugees who entered the United States in 1980. But all who use that figure—often rounding it off to a neat one million—do so knowing it was an extraordinarily unusual year due to the admission of large numbers of Indochinese refugees and the influx of Cubans and Haitians. The numbers before and since are much lower, and will not reach the 1980 level again in the foreseeable future.

We must avoid scare tactics and scare statistics designed to feed false fears.

The bill makes a number of unfortunate and unwise changes in the existing immigration preference system. These changes will jeopardize our country's historic commitment to family reunion as the principal goal of our immigration policy.

For the first time, this bill places the admission of the immediate relatives of United States citizens—spouses, children and parents—under a rigid annual ceiling.

Some very important reforms of the asylum adjudication process have been achieved in this legislation and I support them. However, I regret that the Committee limited judicial review of the asylum process without granting full independence to the new Immigration Board, as originally proposed when the bill was introduced.

I continue to support the unanimous vote of the Select Commission and the actions of the Committee in rejecting the establishment of an expanded temporary foreign worker program. Adoption of the legalization program and implementation of the new immigration system will result in the legal admission of additional immigrants and an adjustment in the status of undocumented aliens already working here.

Until the impact of these changes is assessed, there is no valid justification for a large new temporary foreign worker program. Any such program would have serious consequences for American labor and American wages. The Committee has acted responsibly in rejecting calls for a new "bracero" program.

The existing need for temporary workers can be met by the H-2 visa program. The Committee has acted to make this program more flexible, but we must be extremely cautious not to allow these changes to undermine labor standards or to depress wages. Employers seeking H-2 workers must be required to seek American workers first, and we should plan the elimination of this program in the future, not its expansion.

The Committee bill should be amended to permit students of exceptional merit and ability—who are participating in essential academic, professional and industrial programs—to remain in this country without leaving for two years, and not subject to an arbitrary ceiling. To do otherwise is contrary to our national interests. It also ignores the current reality that exceptionally qualified students do not return to their homes in the Third World or elsewhere; they simply move to Japan or Europe and use their skills to help those nations compete against the United States. It makes no sense, when our faculties and firms are starved for scientific talent, for the United States to train engineers or computer specialists at M.I.T. or Berkeley for jobs in Tokyo or Bonn.

The Select Commission voted unanimously to recommend that a flexible and generous program be established to adjust the status of undocumented aliens already leading productive lives in the United States. It did so because "the existence of a large undocumented/illegal migrant population should not be tolerated"—and because "the costs to society of permitting a large group of persons to live in illegal, second-class status are enormous." The Commission recognized that mass deportations were out of the question, for both legal and humanitarian reasons; such deportations would undermine new enforcement programs and would waste available enforcement resources.

For a legalization program to work, it must be comprehensive, it must reach out to as many undocumented aliens as possible, and it must have as few exceptions as possible.

I regret, therefore, that the Committee did not this year adopt my amendment to make the legalization cut-off date more inclusive—moving it forward from January 1, 1980, to December 31, 1981. Even by the estimates compiled by the Immigration and Naturalization Service this will mean that close to two-thirds of the undocumented aliens in the United States will not be eligible for the legalization program. It means that a large, subterranean, exploited class of people will be left in limbo.

Finally, some concern has been expressed over the impact this legalization program will have on state and local social programs. According to research of the Select Commission and others on the characteristics of the undocumented alien population, these concerns appear to be exaggerated. Undocumented aliens are here to work, not to seek welfare; they are in many respects undocumented taxpayers contributing to the communities in which they live without the benefits of those taxes.

## THE UNEASY IMMIGRATION DEBATE[2]

On a steamy afternoon last June, more people than could be comfortably accommodated were crowded into a wood-paneled meeting room of the Council on Religion and International Affairs (CRIA), a privately-funded, public-spirited organization that occupies a converted town house on Manhattan's East 64th Street. Most of these visitors were middle-aged men and women from church groups, universities, foundations and social action agencies, although there were also a few representatives of business corporations and the press. Having refreshed themselves with white wine and salted peanuts, the guests squeezed into rows of folding chairs to form an earnestly attentive audience beneath the inscrutable gaze of a portrait of Andrew Carnegie whose benefactions created the Council in 1914 under its earlier title of the Church Peace Union.

The topic that afternoon for what CRIA called a "conversation," was related to international affairs in a wide sense. Lawrence H. Fuchs, the 55-year-old Brandeis University political scientist who had been executive director of the staff serving the Select Commission on Immigration and Refugee Policy that was set up by an act of Congress in October 1978, was to speak about the commission's work. These labors, which lasted for two years and included seven public meetings, 12 regional hearings and the sponsorship of an imposing variety of scholarly consultations and special studies, culminated in *U.S. Immigration Policy and the National Interest*, a 453-page report that the 16

[2]Reprint of a magazine article by author and editor John W. Donohue. *America.* 146:206–9. Mr. 20, '82. Reprinted with permission of America Press, Inc., 106 West 56th Street, New York, NY 10019. Copyright © 1982. All rights reserved.

commissioners (four cabinet members, four senators, four from the House and four Presidential appointees) submitted to President Reagan and the Congress on March 1, 1981.

Mr. Fuchs, a trim, dark-haired man with an aquiline profile and the intellectual energy of a first-rate lecturer, made it clear at once that immigration is among the most critical of contemporary global questions. He thinks, as do most people, that the proliferation of nuclear weapons is the world's number one problem and that finding ways of sharing more equitably the earth's food and energy resources is second. But the third major issue, he believes, is precisely the one created by the pressures for migration that people in many countries feel.

Since migration is a world problem, its solution, as the commission pointed out in the opening pages of its report, requires an international effort. "No nation," Lawrence Fuchs said, "can do it all alone." But in no nation is immigration so politically sensitive an issue as it is in the United States. There are two reasons for this. On the one hand, many of those people on the move want to come here. On the other hand, many respectable Americans would like to discourage immigration, even though they are uneasily aware that our national tradition is supposed to have been one of hospitality toward newcomers. They agree with Senator Alan K. Simpson, the rangy and intelligent Republican from Wyoming who is chairman of the Senate's Judiciary Subcommittee on Immigration and Refugee Policy, when he warns that the United States is no longer a developing country that can absorb large numbers of immigrants. That may be true, but it is also paradoxically true that Mr. Simpson happens to represent a state in which a total population of fewer than 500,000 people rattles around in largely empty spaces.

As of January 1981, approximately 1.1 million applicants had registered for immigrant visas at our consular offices abroad. Although the United States' current world-wide annual ceiling for immigrants is a moderate 270,000, the number actually admitted in recent years has been much larger than that. Not only do the immediate relatives (spouses, children and parents) of U.S. citizens constitute a numerically exempt group, but there is also a separate category for political refugees. The freedom flotillas that suddenly took off from Cuba and Haiti in the spring of 1980 sailed into that category, and consequently the overall number of immigrants admitted in 1980 was 808,000.

That figure was greater than the total admitted by all other countries combined. But some further observations are in order. It should be remembered that the United States is not the only country harboring both refugees (who, in theory, are not permanent settlers) and illegal as well as legal immigrants. As Professor Fuchs has pointed out, Somalia, which is a country of 3.6 million people, has been overwhelmed by 1.5 million Ethiopian refugees. And if Mexicans are crossing our southern border to find work, Guatemalans and Salvadorans are crossing Mexico's southern border for the same reason.

Moreover, only 4 or 5 percent of those now living in the United States are foreign born, although 14.7 were in 1910. This percentage is an all-time low, and in a letter to The New York Times last June, the president of the University of Notre Dame, the Rev. Theodore M. Hesburgh, C.S.C., who was chairman of the Select Commission, noted: "Eight other advanced industrial countries (Australia, Switzerland, Canada, New Zealand, South Africa, France, Sweden and Great Britain) currently have a higher percentage of foreign-born than does the United States."

Father Hesburgh added, however, that what alarms many Americans is not the percentage of legal immigrants "but the presence of large numbers of persons who come to the United States outside the law or who abuse their nonimmigrant visas." In a fact sheet issued July 30, 1981, by the Department of Justice as a companion piece to the statement on immigration policy that President Reagan made that same day, it was said: "The Census Bureau has estimated that 3.5 million to 6 million people are in the U.S. illegally—at least 50 percent from Mexico. About 1–1.5 million entered illegally in 1980."

These calculations are highly tentative since undocumented workers naturally do not show up to be counted. But the figures are startling enough to generate a chill, if not a panic, and to make today's citizens forget that they are themselves either immigrants or the descendants of immigrants. It is to Mr. Reagan's credit that in his policy statement last July he did not overlook this significant fact. "Our nation is a nation of immigrants," he began. "More than any other country, our strength comes from our own immigrant heritage and our capacity to welcome those from other lands." And a few lines later, when he listed eight principles that he thinks should govern immigration policy, the President put this in first place: "We shall continue America's tradition as a land that welcomes peoples from other countries. We shall also, with other countries, continue to share in the responsibility of welcoming and resettling those who flee oppression."

Perhaps we shall; one hopes so. When the President's statement was discussed on a telecast of "Agronsky and Company" last summer, the political commentator, Elizabeth Drew, remarked dismissively that it is considered not nice to oppose that hospitable tradition of which Mr. Reagan spoke. And certainly nowadays no politician would complain openly, as Theodore Roosevelt did during World War I, that "hyphenated Americans" are turning the country into a "polyglot boarding house." Nevertheless, a 1980 Roper poll found that not only do nine out of ten Americans want illegal immigration stopped (which is a reasonable desire), but eight out of ten want even legal immigration cut back.

When Mother Teresa visited Miami last June to open one of her congregation's shelters for the poor, she advised Miamians to continue to find room for the Cubans and Haitians who have been pouring into Dade County since 1960. "God must have chosen you for something special," she said, "because at your gates hundreds and hundreds of people have come, and you have not shut your doors."

Lawrence Fuchs could tell Mother Teresa that the people of Miami have also, to use one of his favorite phrases, done well by doing good. The contributions made by immigrants is a theme running through the 916-page Staff Report issued April 30, 1981, as a supplement to the Select Commission's official report two months earlier. This second report, which is stuffed with concrete details, information analyses and excellent tables, is surely the best one-volume survey of American immigration policy and practice. Its fourth chapter, written by Mr. Fuchs himself, summarizes the benefits that the United States has derived from immigrants ("more than 30 percent of the American Nobel prize winners now living are immigrants"), and at one point it quotes a comment Senator William Proxmire (D., Wis.) made after reading a study of the economic impact of Cubans in Miami: "An unprecedented prosperity has been created in Miami as a direct result of its transformation by virtue of the very presence of the Cubans."

But despite the opinions of Mother Teresa and Senator Proxmire, most people in Miami would like to shut their gates, particularly because they blame an increase in crime on the Cubans who arrived in 1980. The Catholic bishops of Florida, who have actively defended the Cuban and Haitian refugees, admitted in a pastoral statement last October that the number and problems of these immigrants make "the American and Christian response extremely difficult in the state of Florida . . . even the American Catholic begins to see in the entrant or refugee not Christ, but the enemy."

This climate of disaffection, if not hostility, provides public officials with cues. Although President Reagan's policy statement took high ground and was affirmative in tone, most of his Administration's specific proposals have been preoccupied with the negative business of controlling the flow of illegal aliens and they have the tone of a householder who thinks new arrivals are ruining the neighborhood.

Summarizing these plans in testimony last summer before a joint meeting of the Senate and House subcommittees on immigration, U.S. Attorney General William French Smith echoed the phrase so popular with editorialists: "We have lost control of our borders."

No doubt, the Attorney General's use of the plural was diplomatic. Undocumented Canadians are not streaming across the northern boundary. It was obviously the southern border that Mr. Smith had in mind, but today Washington takes more care to avoid offending Mexican sensibilities than it once did. Haiti inspires no similar caution, and the Administration's new policy has included such hobnailed police actions as the interdicting, even in international waters, of boats suspected of smuggling Haitians into South Florida and the holding of Haitian refugees in miserable detention centers.

Even legal immigration, however, makes some public officeholders restive enough to argue that the national tradition of hos-

pitality should be curtailed, if not abandoned. Governor Richard
D. Lamm of Colorado, for example, made that genial view clear
in "America Needs Fewer Immigrants," an essay he contributed
to the op-ed page of The New York Times on July 12, 1981. As
children or grandchildren of immigrants, the Governor wrote, we
are blinded by our past myths and now "we have to get our hearts
in line with our heads and our myths in line with reality." Once
we have accomplished this bit of ideological chiropractic, we will
see, Mr. Lamm thinks, that we must set strict limits on immigration, even if this seems selfish: "Our immigration policy has to be
designed in the interests of the United States."

Senator Simpson has views much like those of Governor
Lamm and in his position as chairman of the subcommittee on immigration, he is currently playing a key role in the designing of
a new immigration law. The Senator was also a member of the
Select Commission, and some idea of his thinking can be gathered
from what he had to say in that final report of the commission.
The main text of this document, which is the reproduction of a
typescript, takes up 298 pages and is followed by 10 appendices.
The second, and by far the longest, of these runs to 92 rather con-
tentious pages in which 12 of the 16 commissioners file supple-
mentary statements of dissent from one or many of the
approximately 80 recommendations adopted by a majority vote.

In his vigorous and detailed statement, Senator Simpson confi-
dently observes that Americans are more compassionate than any
other people. Indeed, their virtue is so excessive that they are inevitably suffering from what Mr. Simpson calls "compassion
fatigue." Before proposing remedies for this distress, the Senator
remarks that what he has to say may be misunderstood. But he
need not have feared; his position is clear enough. "Immigrants
can still greatly benefit America," he writes, "but only if they are
limited to an appropriate number and selected within that number
on the basis of traits which would truly benefit America."

Appropriate selection, it turns out, means fewer immigrants
from Latin America. Senator Simpson puts it plainly:
"Immigration to the United States is now dominated to a high degree by persons speaking a single foreign language, Spanish, when
illegal immigration is considered. The assimilation of the English

language and other aspects of American culture by Spanish-speaking immigrants appears to be less rapid and complete than for other groups. . . . If immigration is continued at a high level and yet a substantial portion of the newcomers and their descendants do not assimilate, they may create in America some of the same social, political and economic problems which existed in the country which they have chosen to depart."

Spokesmen for the various Hispanic communities in the United States might want to ask Senator Simpson just what ominous problems he foresees. Many may be only mirages. For instance, some observers think Mexican-American families are too large, but studies reviewed for the Select Commission show that fertility among Mexican Americans decreases as the time they live here lengthens and their socioeconomic status rises.

But if some of Senator Simpson's sociological opinions are arguable, his conviction that the United States needs to overhaul its immigration policy is not. There would never have been a Select Commission had this necessity for reform not been generally recognized. At a national conference on immigration held in San Diego last June, Representative Romano L. Mazzoli, the Kentucky Democrat who as chairman of the House subcommittee on immigration is Senator Simpson's opposite number, said: "Today's immigration law is really no law at all; it is unenforceable." At the same meeting, Mr. Simpson said that people who are alarmed by the numbers even of legal immigrants, are writing him letters that boil down to "What are you boobs going to do?"

In New York City a few weeks ago, Mr. Simpson met with several groups to explain exactly what he and Mr. Mazzoli would be doing about immigration this month. The day began with an 8:30 press breakfast (coffee and danish) in the conference room of the Carnegie Endowment for International Peace on the 54th floor of 30 Rockefeller Plaza. After remarking that he had come to town "to discuss the value of rural America with Mayor Ed Koch," whose disparagement of country life had recently been making lively headlines, Senator Simpson spoke briefly about two bills that will be submitted to Congress. This first is a so-called "core" bill that provides some immediate measures for controlling illegal immigration and that would be introduced, the Senator said, on March 10. Later on, there will be a comprehensive bill that completely rewrites the current law which is the 1952 Immigration and Nationality (McCarran-Walter) Act as revised in 1965 and 1976. The time has come, Mr. Simpson indicated, for immigration reform. On the Senate floor, he said, his colleagues often stop to ask him when they can expect his bill and as for the nation itself: "There have never been more constituent groups out there wanting us to do something."

One of the main things we have to do, the Senator added, is "to learn to say no and to get over the guilt trip about saying no." This advice points up the first of the major questions that any new immigration policy must answer: How many people should be admitted for permanent residency each year?

Immigrants, as distinguished from the 11 million tourists and commercial travelers who visit this country annually, come to the United States for one or more of three principal reasons: to join members of their family already here, to improve their economic condition, or to escape persecution. Since the United States is theoretically an open society, these newcomers ought always to have been admitted to citizenship without prolonged delay and without having been sifted through a discriminatory network of racial, ethnic or religious qualifications. In historic practice, however, immigration policy was for 150 years more or less compromised by the nativism that is the American version of humanity's ancient distrust of the stranger.

The current immigration law, as the Select Commission's staff report notes, "is far more equitable than its predecessors . . . but the basic blueprint itself—a numerical limit on immigration, a preference system combining family and worker priorities, some sort of limit on the number of immigrants admissible from any one country, and exemption of certain groups of immediate relatives and 'special' immigrants from these limits—remains essentially the same."

In making their own proposals, the Administration, Senator Simpson and Representative Mazzoli, and the Select Commission have all retained this basic blueprint, but they vary its details. The Simpson-Mazzoli bill, for instance, would set 425,000 as the maximum number of immigrants to be admitted in any one year. Since reunification of families is the first aim of any humane policy, the immediate relatives of U.S. citizens would continue to have unrestricted entry, but they would be included in the computation of that maximum or "cap" of 425,000. Refugees would be admitted under the separate heading of the 1980 Refugees Act, but it is assumed that normally they would not exceed 50,000 a year and that many of them would intend returning when possible to their homeland.

The Select Commission, encouraged no doubt by its staff, took a truly comprehensive view of immigration policy and did not concentrate exclusively on the question of controlling the borders. It understood that a really adequate policy must be a viable synthesis of those two great ideals which the staff report calls the principle of the open society and the principle of the rule of the law, the ideal of hospitality and the ideal of legal control. The commission recognized, as Mr. Fuchs put it in one of the chapters he contributed to the staff report, that "the open society does not mean limitless immigration. Both quantitative and qualitative limits are needed to serve the national interests of the United States."

But the more one understands and appreciates the ideal of the open society, the more generously and subtly one will judge of those limits. The commission, therefore, called for opening the front door a bit wider by raising the annual ceiling on numerically restricted immigration to 350,000 with an additional 100,000 visas allowed for the first five years in order to clear the present backlog of applications. In order to preserve what it called cultural diversity and fairness toward all nations, the commission recommended a per-country ceiling, although it recognized that the number of Mexicans wanting to emigrate will greatly exceed that fixed percentage, whereas the number of British, for example, will fall short of the limit. However, the commission also proposed that the immediate relatives of American citizens be exempted from numerical limitations. Allowing for refugees, therefore, the commission envisioned an annual total gross immigration of 670,000. A total emigration of about 30 percent, or 176,000 would reduce net immigration to 494,000.

The commissioners knew, however, that even this relatively modest quota for legal immigrants will be opposed unless ways can be found for shutting off the flow of illegal aliens. That is to say, the principle of the rule of law has to be integrated with the principle of the open society, and the immigration debate is uneasy because this integration is so difficult. The commissioners and the staff were perfectly aware of the tension between these two ideals. For instance, Lawrence Fuchs and his assistants met with some of those undocumented workers and found them, as he told the CRIA audience, "beautiful and above-average people who were self-selected for a certain amount of risk-taking and creativity." If they had not been adventuresome, they would never have tried to cross the border in the first place. Those risks they run have become the stuff of legend and have inspired not only Jack Nicholson's new movie, "The Border," but also a number of television dramas including an episode of "The Incredible Hulk" last fall [1981].

When Mr. Fuchs joined the Immigration and Naturalization Service's border patrol on one of its nighttime sweeps along the Rio Grande, he found the experience disturbing. "I flew in the helicopter," he said. "I manned the searchlight. And all I kept seeing was my own grandmother down there, my grandmother who came here when she was 16 and spent several days of frightening interrogation on Ellis Island."

At the same time he recognized, as he said, that "we can't go on making a travesty of our immigration policy by not enforcing the regulations." This recognition is general and has produced four proposals to which, with many individual qualifications, the Administration, the Select Commission, and the sponsors of the Simpson-Mazzoli bill all subscribe.

The serious social problem created by the presence of a harried underclass of millions of illegal aliens would be cured by legitimizing the status of all those undocumented immigrants who were here as of Jan. 1, 1980. Through this amnesty they could, sooner or later, acquire citizenship. But amnesty without new enforcement measures would, as Lawrence Fuchs has said, be mere forgiveness and might be interpreted as a reward for illegality. The Select Commission, therefore, made three recommendations that Senator Simpson has compared to the legs of a stool: "If we lose one of them, the game is over."

The Immigration and Naturalization Service must be given far greater funds so that it can patrol the border both more efficiently and more justly. But the prospective illegal immigrant, who is typically a young, unmarried man, won't be much tempted to cross that border in the first place, if he can't expect to find work here. U.S. employers, says the staff report, have consistently perpetuated illegal migration. They will reform their ways, however, once a reciprocal system of employee eligibility/employer responsibility has been set up. When this is in place, employers hiring undocumented workers will be liable to civil and even to criminal sanctions.

Such sanctions cannot be imposed, however, unless every job-seeking American can be identified as eligible for employment. How this is to be done is anxiously disputed. The Administration favors the use of existing identifiers like the Social Security card or a driver's license. The Select Commission and Senator Simpson think some new, counterfeit-proof form of national identification is needed and could be devised without turning the Federal Government into Big Brother.

If there is to be a full-scale debate of immigration policy, these specific measures and a complex bundle of others are likely to monopolize the discussion. That is unfortunate but probably inevitable. Even the Select Commission, as Lawrence Fuchs has said, was preoccupied with the rule of law. But it was not so preoccupied as to forget the ideal of the open society.

Anyone who realizes that there is much more to immigration reform than transferring some of the Army's helicopters to the use of the Border Patrol, could gain a clear view of wider horizons by reading the Select Commission's two reports. But those unwieldy volumes are no more apt to be found in the neighborhood public library than is a Gutenberg Bible. The libraries could, however, post on their bulletin boards these sentences that Father Hesburgh shrewdly quoted in his introduction to *U.S. Immigration Policy and the National Interest*. They are from the speech Ronald Reagan gave in 1980 when he accepted the Republican nomination for the Presidency: "I ask you to trust that American spirit which knows no ethnic, religious, social, political, regional or economic boundaries: the spirit that burned with zeal in the hearts of mil-

lions of immigrants from every corner of the earth who came here
in search of freedom. . . . Can we doubt that only a divine Provi-
dence placed this land—this island of freedom—here as a refuge
for all those people in the world who yearn to breathe free?"

## U.S. IMMIGRATION POLICY AND THE NATIONAL INTEREST[3]

The security of the United States has suffered in the past as
a result of the government's impotency in the face of massive illegal immigration, and it will continue to suffer as the situation increasingly worsens. Employment levels, domestic political
cohesion, national resources, and the global standing of the United
States can all be adversely affected by the current state of U.S. immigration policy. If these concerns are not addressed forthwith,
there is a real danger that relative government inaction will be followed by public overreaction.

One of the primary reasons for the lack of attention paid to
effective immigration policy in the past is the sensitivity of the subject. After all, the imageries of the United States as a nation of immigrants are both powerful and accurate. The very fabric of
American society has been affected by it. However, these imageries most likely refer to a world environment that no longer exists. The extent of annual illegal immigration into the United
States—approximately 650,000 in lean years—and the political,
economic, and social ramifications suggest a dangerous anomaly.
A gap has developed between the symbols of a "nation of
immigrants" and the realities of the "huddled masses yearning to
be free."

In focusing on the significance of immigration policy to the national interest of the United States, it is necessary to note two aspects of recent U.S. immigration policy that adversely affect the

[3] Reprint of a magazine article by Georges Fauriol, a professor at Georgetown University's Center for Strategic and International Studies. This article first appeared in *The Humanist*, issue of May/June 1984 (44:5), and is reprinted by permission.

security and development of *other* nations. The "drain" of skilled professionals and proponents of political freedom from many Third World nations, encouraged in large part by U.S. immigration policy, undermines the human pool of political and economic talent of those countries. Conceivably, it enriches our own. The irony is that the economic and political changes required of Third World countries are likely to be delayed if migration to the United States remains an integral aspect of Third World development policy.

Looking over the horizon, the implications of this for the United States are serious though uncertain. As this country speeds toward the twenty-first century, one has to express considerable alarm at the laid-back attitude regarding migration flows to American shores. The linkage with foreign policy and national security is not always a direct one: it is a delicate process, and, above all, one difficult to articulate. To dismiss a relationship between immigration and foreign and security policies suggests ignorance of the interrelationships present in the world today—a world whose future trends will not always be favorable to the United States.

## A Glance to the Future

Few politicians see any political capital in the immigration policy issue. As an editorial writer in *The Journal of Commerce* put it recently, "Immigration policy has little appeal for most politicians. While they are not unaware of the disastrous long-run consequences of doing nothing, they see nothing but grief in taking action now." Current U.S. immigration policy is a national disgrace. The beneficiaries of this policy remain politically powerful, unwilling to put aside narrow, special interests for the national good. Those pushing for reform, while enjoying overwhelming public support, do not have sufficient financial or organizational clout to effectively translate this support into action.

The long-run implications of our current "head in the sand" attitude about maintaining de facto open borders are indeed serious. They go to the heart of our security as a nation, our domestic political unity, our economic prosperity, and our role in the international system. Illegal immigration is by its very nature causing pressures beyond those associated with heavy immigration flows in particular and population growth in general.

Opposition to "open borders" or support for immigration reform has for too long been erroneously characterized as representative of a return to "nativism," of an emerging racism. This has led to an unwillingness to examine the more serious and important aspects of U.S. immigration policy.

Though we cannot predict the future, we can, with a certain amount of common sense, glance toward the turn to the twenty-first century and see what the national landscape would look like without modification of U.S. immigration policy. It is from this perspective that immigration policy should probably be shaped. This involves not only an examination of the effects of illegal immigration today but, more importantly, forecasting what the future will bring if the pressures persist.

First, what portion of the 800 to 900 million new job seekers in the developing world between 1980 and 2000 will the United States be forced to accept as a result of porous borders?

Second, will the 15 million Americans earning minimum wages, who compete directly with many illegal aliens for employment, be better or worse off if the system of illegal immigration continues and worsens?

Third, will respect for the laws of the United States, for the integrity of its national sovereignty, be strengthened by perpetuating a weak system of immigration law enforcement?

Fourth, will creation of enclaves of often second-class citizens, speaking only their native tongue, contribute to the political and linguistic cohesion of the country?

Fifth, will the blurring of the distinction between citizen and noncitizen, between lawful and unlawful resident, undermine the integrity of the electoral process and the legal fabric that holds the nation together?

Sixth, will immigration at current levels (nearly 1.5 million annually) contribute to the energy security of the United States, when projections indicate that the growth from legal immigration alone from 1982 to 1992 could consume an amount of energy costing $88 billion annually?

Seventh, will the addition of tens of millions of immigrants to the country over the next few generations improve our chances to conserve our natural resources, reduce our foreign oil dependence, and secure a high standard of living at a sustainable resource use rate?

Finally, will U.S. foreign policy remain coherent and independent and able to best serve the national interest if the decisions concerning who enters this country and uses its resources are strongly influenced by other governments and their populations?

These are serious questions. To dismiss them is shortsighted and would, in fact, suggest that the United States has the luxury of choice and time regarding immigration policy concerns. The new international environment of the 1980s, the recent energy crises, the vulnerable American hold on the global financial system, and the changing structure of the United States domestic economy may imply the opposite. The manner in which immigration and refugee considerations interact in the above mix cannot be underestimated.

Without sovereign control over national borders, the United States can lose control over the size and nature of its labor force, population size, and linguistic and political unity. Furthermore, the size of the nation's population will determine the adequacy of natural resources and the extent to which damages to the environment can be mitigated. This in turn will influence the productivity of the economy and the ability of the United States to compete successfully internationally. Finally, U.S. foreign policy may be greatly undermined by a continuation of the currently fluid nature of immigration policy; foreign powers will increasingly use the emigration threat to induce U.S. concessions or threaten retaliation should the United States move to strengthen its immigration statutes.

The nature of immigration policy can most likely no longer remain the exclusive domain of current dominant special interests. All things considered, immigration policy must be related to broad economic, demographic, and foreign policy themes. As was pointed out in "Illegal Immigration: Challenge to the United States" (a report of the Immigration Policy Panel of the Economic Policy Council of the UNA-USA, December 1981), "Control over entry by noncitizens is one of the two or three universal attributes of nation states."

While much attention has been paid to the domestic economic impacts of immigration, little has been said concerning its relationship with the emerging international economic and political context in which the United States finds itself. In addition, the disruptive effects of uncontrolled immigration on the political unity of the nation has also largely been ignored. The evidence is very strong that the international push factors generating illicit and legal immigration are among the most powerful contemporary factors in international affairs. Thus, the context in which traditional or historical migration to the United States has occurred is no longer relevant to the current global situation. The myths of the past must be discarded for the realities of the present.

U.S. international economic policy and success in competing overseas will depend in large part upon increases in U.S. economic productivity, including a highly trained work force, and increased business investment. Immigration, both legal and illegal, may in the future create a permanent underclass of unskilled workers, many of whom will remain unemployed.

Also, there is a concern that the growing use of racial or ethnic political power blocs in the United States will foster a divisiveness within American society. This issue is not stated here lightly. Since the 1970s, for example, bilingualism has become a highly visible public agenda in schools, governments, and media. Its relationship with present trends of large migration flows of people from Spanish-speaking countries is obvious. Ethnic power group manipulation of U.S. foreign policy is nothing new. Will a nation divided along ethnic or linguistic lines be a united nation, able to carry on a bipartisan and consistent foreign policy?

Finally, uncontrolled immigration is resulting in foreign countries using migration as a foreign policy weapon. Cuba and Vietnam, most notably, have sent their political dissidents, criminals, and espionage agents to the United States in the knowledge that the U.S. government is currently unable to control immigration into this country. Furthermore, hostile governments are patently aware of the destabilizing effects such influxes may have on the "recipient countries," thereby enabling them to create a massive liability for their opposition.

*The New Migration: The Population Bomb Rediscovered*

Because of the rich folklore surrounding the question of immigration, it is difficult to come to grips with the new realities that confront the United States. As a result, current U.S. immigration policy remains rooted in the convenient mythology of the nineteenth century.

When the United States was empty, with no functional frontiers, it needed immigrants to fill the continent. Those days are gone, yet the myth lingers on. The vast continent is now filled with migrants from every corner of the globe. America's bounty has been replaced by dramatically high unemployment, scarce supplies of natural resources, severe problems of economic productivity, and divisions within the social fabric.

So, too, has the entire world changed. Instead of 1 billion, the world population now exceeds 4.8 billion. The Brandt Commission and the *Global 2000 Report* have warned of the growing incompatibility between increased numbers of people, the supporting natural resource base, and environmental deterioration. Endemic poverty, historically unprecedented levels of unemployment, and related political and civil unrest are emerging as major world forces, with massive international migration a prominent result.

In the developing world, there are over 3.5 billion people. The populations of Panama, Costa Rica, El Salvador, Guatemala, Nicaragua, and Honduras, for example, have grown from 9 million in 1950 to nearly 25 million today; by the year 2000, the numbers will have swelled to 40 million and then to 70 million by the year 2025. The potential migrants to the United States through the rest of the century have already been born; over the next two decades, they will emerge into the labor force of the Third World nations with an explosive power far beyond anything previously experienced by humankind. Those people born between now and the end of the century are simply the tidal wave of the labor force explosion of the twenty-first century.

The annual growth in the populations of the Third World nations from which illegal and legal immigrants are coming has not receded—in fact, the annual increase in both overall population and the labor force has continued to increase in gross numbers throughout this period. For example, in 1963 it was projected that Mexico's population by 1980 would grow to 70.6 million; the actual number reached was nearly 72 million, not including the suspected 3 to 4 million Mexicans living in the United States illegally. With respect to the labor force, the region of Central America and the Caribbean as well as South America is adding 4.5 million people to its labor force every year. Though the region has only one-third the overall GNP the United States has, it adds twice as many workers to its working-age population every year.

Even in the face of these increasingly worrisome push factors, important elements of American society continue to press for open borders. For example, Atlantic Richfield's executive vice-president, Ralph Cocks, states that, because Mexico has "all that population growth," they must have an outlet. The United States, says Cocks, "is a natural outlet in that we will have a labor shortage in the next two decades." Similarly, the United Methodist's Council of Bishops has requested that the United States impose no numerical limitations on immigration from Mexico and Canada, make all public services available to illegal residents, and allow employers to continue to hire those unlawfully in the United States. In addition, the Institute for Policy Studies is organizing what it terms "Third World communities" in the United States around immigration issues, asserting that people have the "right to emigrate" to the United States. In effect, these organizations, and many like them, are threatening the security of the United States.

## Implications for the United States

There is undisputed evidence that the flow of both legal and illegal immigration, including border crossings and overstays, is increasing dramatically. For example, twenty years ago, the total number of apprehended aliens seeking admission to the United States was under 40,000 per year. By 1970, that number had grown to over 260,000, and by the end of 1983 had grown in excess of 1.3 million. It is indicative of the unfortunate state of current U.S. immigration policy that the number of agents on duty at any one time actively seeking to stop illegal migration has gone up only marginally throughout this same period.

One of the more unfortunate assumptions concerning illicit migration is the view that it is largely a Mexican-United States phenomenon; although apprehensions along the U.S. border are concentrated in the Southwest and predominantly involve Mexico, illegal immigrants come to the United States from at least sixty different countries, according to the 1978 report of the Select Committee on Population and Immigration policy. Although the U.S.-Canadian border is only lightly patroled, apprehensions of illegal immigrants in this sector are up 70 percent over 1982 levels, with people from China, West Germany, Greece, Haiti, Poland, Nigeria, Canada, and Latin American nations apprehended.

Legal immigration has continued to grow as well, with legal Mexican migration more than doubling from 70,000 in 1973 to 150,000 in 1983. Overall, legal immigration reached the 800,000 mark in 1980 and has since topped 600,000 in each of the following years, a 50 percent increase over the average increase in population attributed to immigration for the decade of the 1970s.

The implications of such growth for the demographic future of the United States are vastly more serious than most observers have acknowledged. The U.S. population, while projected to grow to 250 million by the year 2000 without immigration, will reach nearly 270 million with an annual immigration rate of 600,000. These numbers also assume a continued low U.S. fertility rate (1.8). If U.S. fertility rates climb to 2.0, however, the U.S. population will grow to nearly 270 million even with zero net immigration. Despite the awareness among most Americans of the need to exercise responsible parenthood and the trend toward limiting family size to two children or less, immigration is effectively cancelling the positive impact such a fertility reduction would otherwise have.

The massive impact immigration can have on the ultimate size of the U.S. population can be seen when projected out to the year 2080, a century hence: without immigration exceeding emigration, the U.S. population would be about 250 million *and declining*; but with immigration at 2 million a year, the population would be *558 million and growing rapidly*. (An often overlooked point is that projections of U.S. population growth made by the U.S. Bureau of Census, and thus viewed as official, assume immigration at 400,000 annually and emigration at 150,000 annually. The emigration numbers are purely speculative; there are no data on emigration from the United States which justify the assumption that such a large number of Americans are migrating abroad, particularly on a permanent basis. The population numbers also assume that recent immigrants will maintain a fertility rate similar to the U.S. native population, an assumption not warranted by the facts.)

### National Political Cohesion

Much of the debate concerning illegal immigration has centered on the displacement of extant American workers and tax revenues which are foregone. However, there are unique dimensions to the current immigration that have the potential to severely disrupt the political cohesion of the country. Illegal immigration, by virtue of its current size, and because of its concentration among Hispanics, is leading to three fundamental conflicts within American society.

First, the push for bilingual education has centered on the interest and needs of the Hispanic population in the United States. This issue raises a much broader issue. As columnist and political commentator Tom Braden wrote in *The Washington Times* on August 23, 1983:

Do we want a country unified by a common tongue? Or do we want a country made separate but equal by having to deal in two? I worry about it. Is it prejudice that reminds me that, throughout two hundred odd years, we have been the gainers by having only one?

Second, there is increasing recognition of the potential political clout of the Hispanic population. As a result of high native fertility and large-scale legal and illegal immigration, the U.S. Hispanic population is increasing rapidly. By virtue of the size of the population, attempts can be made to secure political favors. (The National Council of La Raza has claimed that Hispanics will be the largest minority in the country by 1990 and, by virtue of this supposition, should be accorded substantial political benefits.) This can foster a tendency to cater to "Hispanic" interests as somehow distinct from those of other Americans. And to the extent to which the political clout of Hispanics is fueled by open-ended illegal immigration, U.S. sovereignty over its borders can conceivably be influenced by the political expediency of ethnic politics.

Third, a related but perhaps even more profound development flows from the growing numbers of illegal immigrants. Because political representation and the disbursement of substantial amounts of federal funds is based upon population, the 1980 census made major efforts to include illegal immigrants. To the extent that illegal immigrants increase the population of any particular state, their relative political representation is increased as is their receipt of federal dollars. This suggests a skewed system in which there might be little incentive for states to work *against* the inclusion of illegal immigrants or *for* the reform of immigration statutes, if by the presence of large numbers of illegal immigrants they gain in tax revenues and political clout.

The viability of the nation depends upon an informed electorate and the absence of deep cultural or lingual divisions among its people. Illegal immigration, to the extent that it fosters the establishment of communities of persons unable or unwilling to converse in English, can foster just such divisions. The problem of a large ethnic group, repeatedly fueled by massive immigration—whether legal or illegal—detached from the mainstream U.S. population by language and custom, "could effect the social stability of the nation," says William A. Henry III in *Time* (June 13, 1983). He continues:

The disruptive potential of bilingualism and biculturalism is worrisome: millions of voters cut off from the main sources of information, millions of potential draftees inculcated with dual ethnic loyalties, millions of would-be employees ill at ease in the language of their workmates.

According to a study prepared by the Twentieth Century Fund, bilingual education, on which the U.S. government spends nearly $200 million annually, does not assist in creating a better society but just the opposite. "Anyone living in the United States who is unable to speak English cannot fully participate in our society, its culture, its politics" says the Fund's task force, recommending that funds currently being used for bilingual education be used to assist non-English-speaking children to learn to speak, read, and write in English. Congressman Kiki de la Garza expressed this concern in testimony before the U.S. Supreme Court: "Uncontrolled immigration is threatening the quality of education we can provide our children. . . . Many alien immigrant children have little if any command of the English language and little familiarity with our American customs and traditions, making personalized attention very important," thus placing great burdens on the local school.

Bilingualism fueled by massive immigration flows has unintended consequences as well. In Miami, many of the city's blacks are unable to find work because they do not speak Spanish, a prerequisite for holding a job in many Miami area hotels, stores, and restaurants.

Since its birth, the United States has sought to maintain a linguistic unity. Our founding fathers were well aware of the conflicts and disunity which were bred by religious and linguistic differences. The United States has been blessed with a common language through which political, social, and economic discourse can be conducted. Illegal immigration is a grave threat to that unity, particularly when it is associated with pressures to provide bilingual education in America's primary school systems. Bilingualism does not strengthen the ability of groups to communicate with each other and build social cohesion. As commentator Eric Sevareid has said, bilingualism could "produce greater strain on this country than black-white relations."

## Blurred Citizenship and the Illegal Immigrant

1980 may be remembered by future historians as a watershed date in American history. For the first time, the U.S. government made a major effort to include illegal immigrants in the National Census. The census not only influences the distribution of federal tax dollars but is fundamental to the apportionment process which determines the number of representatives each state is entitled to have in the U.S. Congress. During the process of a lawsuit brought by the Federation for American Immigration Reform to block this inclusion, it was pointed out that the inclusion of millions of illegal aliens in the census would deprive certain states of representatives to which they otherwise would be entitled, while other states would unfairly gain additional representatives.

Unfortunately, an end to illegal immigration and the curtailment of legal immigration to reasonable levels may be perceived in the future as a threat by the beneficiaries of this growing political clout. Illegal immigration, to the extent that it fuels an increasing number of insular ethnic groups, becomes a tool with which to persuade government policymakers to look favorably upon the demands of ethnic organizations, which could include the maintenance of open borders. This has been most notably demonstrated by the recent action of Tip O'Neill, speaker of the U.S. House of Representatives, in pulling the Immigration Reform Bill off the House calendar. (He has since changed his mind, and the bill is back on the calendar.)*

By including illegal immigrants in the census, the U.S. government legitimizes the use of illegal immigration itself as a political tool for the advancement of certain interests in American society. This is certainly not without significant implications for the future of American democracy. The political use of illegal aliens has included attempts by certain states, particularly California, to make major efforts to register illegal aliens to vote. During the Carter administration, the Justice Department informally ruled that it saw no legal reason why illegal aliens could not vote even in federal elections!

It is clear that the right to vote has to be synonymous with the rights of citizenship. Once the distinction becomes blurred between the rights reserved for Americans as opposed to those enjoyed by any newcomer who happens to be lucky enough or careful enough to enter the United States illegally and remain here, the very notion that the United States should have immigration statutes, let alone the right to enforce them, is undermined. The concept of "de facto citizens" implies a legal situation in which the United States has both a political and a moral imperative to grant the rights and privileges enjoyed by the rest of American society to those entering illegally. This is an uncomfortable situation, to say the least.

*The Immigration Reform and Control bill was passed by the House in June 1984.

*Immigration and Employment: Disquieting Trends*

This country retains a chronically high unemployment rate. To the surprise of many, immigration has become a disquieting factor in American economic life: although 2 million new jobs were created each year during the 1970s, half of them went to legal and illegal immigrants; at the same time, unemployment among Hispanics, blacks, teenagers, and women climbed to between 12 and 22 percent. One has to speculate as to the ways this affects the very foundations of this nation.

Critics contend that Americans have always made good use of its immigrant labor to do its "dirty work." This contention, however, evades the issue: is the United States to perpetuate the working conditions that surround this "dirty work" simply to attract illegal immigrants? What happens when such illegal immigrants wish to move on to better paying positions? Does the United States simply increase the flow of further illegal immigrants to take their place? Should the United States continue to tolerate the impact the presence of such an illicit work force has on U.S. workers and the consequent use of tax-supported services that such toleration entails? Is it in the national interest to perpetuate a situation in which the terms of labor competition are "who will work the longest hours, for the lowest pay, and under the most arbitrary conditions?" These are all serious questions.

In the meantime, the assumption that illegal immigration is predominantly a problem of the agricultural sectors of the U.S. economy stubbornly clings to the national conscience. Most internal enforcement of U.S. immigration statutes takes place in agricultural areas, where legal restrictions have not yet limited the impact the Immigration and Naturalization Service can have. In widespread areas of the U.S. economy, little if any attempt has been made to arrest the employment of illegal immigrants. As a result, the problem fades from public view, is ignored by the media, and only occasionally pierces the national conscience.

While the myth endures, the evidence is markedly to the contrary. A 1979 San Diego County study found that the overwhelming number of working illegal immigrants were in construction, manufacturing, retailing, and service industries, with only 7 to 8 percent in agricultural work. (These data are confirmed by over a decade of INS enforcement efforts at employment sites around the country.) In the same study, it was found that between 60 and 80 percent of the illegal immigrants were holding jobs which Americans would take, with 90 to 93 percent of all construction and manufacturing jobs held by aliens falling into that category.

• In one survey in Chicago, illegal immigrants were found to average $9,000 a year, while in Denver the average wage was over $13,000. These people work in "electronics and plastic companies, foundries, meat-packing plants, rubber products manufacturers, snack food and candy producers, and the like," attests John Crewdson of the *New York Times*.

• One-third of all the workers in commercial construction in Houston have been found to be illegally employed, earning from $4.00 to $9.50 per hour, or up to $20,000 annually, according to a Rice University study in January 1982.

• In Elgin, Illinois, the Illinois Department of Labor had no trouble filling openings left after Immigration and Naturalization Service agents arrested sixty-nine workers earning between $3.50 and $14.00 per hour; within hours, hundreds of local residents applied for these jobs, all of which were filled within three days.

• As a result of "Operation Jobs," conducted during the spring of 1982, important additional information became available on the extent of illegal immigration and its impact on employment. Though the average wage of those immigrants apprehended was $4.81 per hour, in both Denver and Chicago wages reached as high as $10.00 per hour.

There may be a small kernel of truth in the assertion that some unskilled jobs which Americans will not do are those taken or filled by illegal immigrants. The major reason for the poor working conditions and poor wages for these jobs is that these conditions are maintained illegally; the general impression is that illegal immigrants holding these jobs will not complain due to fear that they will be turned over to the U.S. Border Patrol or Immigration and Naturalization Service. For while it is illegal for these individuals to work in the United States, it is not illegal for U.S. employers to hire them. Thus, the very illegality of the immigrants contributes to the maintenance of the very working conditions that cause U.S. workers to shun such employment.

One of the chief problems the United States faces is a work force trained for a number of tasks which are declining in demand, while at the same time new technologies and trading needs require different employment skills and knowledge. As entry-level jobs decrease, particularly as automation increases, the kind of jobs most attractive to immigrants, especially illegal immigrants, will not be available, further exacerbating the competition between and among entry-level job-seekers in American society. The potential cost of such competition is substantial. If but 2 million Americans are displaced, the annual cost (in transfer payments) is estimated to be $14 billion. If indeed up to 3.5 percentage points of our national unemployment rate stems from the presence of illegal immigration, then much of the immigration debate appears shallow and beside the point—if any other single factor in American society could be identified with unemployment of such magnitude, it would be at the top of the national political agenda. Regrettably, immigration policy is not.

### Free Lunch Mythology: Taxes and Immigration

It is widely assumed that illegal immigrants seldom use social services and, thus, contribute a greater amount of tax revenues than they receive in benefits. Furthermore, it is asserted that, despite any displacement impact such immigrants may have on U.S. labor force employment, their contributions to the tax base of the society are sufficiently large so as to justify their continued presence within American society.

Evidence is accumulating that points to the conclusion that illegal immigrants may in fact utilize transfer payment services as readily as Americans. Tax-supported services such as sanitation, public transportation, education, environmental cleanup, municipal services—including fire and police protection—and a host of other related services are all utilized by people living in America simply by virtue of their presence here.

In this context, one of the most prevalent myths with respect to illegal immigration is the contention that these workers pay substantial amounts of taxes but receive relatively little in the form of transfer payments such as food stamps, Social Security, or Medicare. However, recent evidence strongly suggests that the extent of the use of transfer payment services is far greater than was previously assumed. First, displaced American workers cost the U.S. treasury substantial amounts of revenue, both in lost taxes and transfer payment benefits. Second, a certain percentage of illegal immigrants work completely off the books and avoid paying taxes altogether. Third, to the extent that illegal immigrant workers are paid below the minimum wage, tax receipts that are collected are reduced. Fourth, a certain percentage of the income of illegal immigrant workers is sent to their native lands, which results in a reduction in purchases and spending in the United States and, consequently, a further reduction in tax revenues. Finally, many illegal immigrant workers have been found to file fraudulent tax returns, claiming dependents in excess of the number allowed and receiving funds when taxes are already underpaid.

Illegal immigrants incur other costs to society as well. In some instances, as with health and educational services, the costs can be particularly heavy due to the low-income characteristics of the illegal alien population. For example:

• A screening of applicants for AFDC food stamps in Los Angeles found 17,000 individuals who withdrew their application when told that the INS would be notified—of those who persisted in applying, 90 percent were found to be illegal immigrants.

• In Illinois, it was found that 45 percent of applicants for unemployment insurance were illegal immigrants.

• Los Angeles County concluded that 1.1 million illegal aliens were costing the county over $629 million annually to educate and provide judicial, health, and other county services.

• Health care costs are escalating as illegal immigrants bear children in U.S. hospitals: in 1981, 81 percent of all children born in just one Denver hospital were to illegal aliens. The resultant health-care costs are enormous.

• For every 1 million Americans that are unemployed, it costs the federal government nearly $25 billion in lost revenues, lost economic activity, and increased expenditures for such things as unemployment compensation, food stamps, and welfare. With only

3 million illegal immigrants considered employed in positions which could eventually be opened up to unemployed Americans, the cost to the American tax payers would be $75 billion. Professor Donald Huddle of Rice University has estimated that, for every one hundred illegal immigrants employed in the United States, seventy U.S. workers are displaced. Every displaced U.S. worker costs $7,000 in transfer or support payments.

## U.S. Foreign Policy, National Security, and the New Immigration

Already the issues of immigration and refugee policies have acted as substantial destabilizing forces in the already precarious North-South relationship. These issues feed on the larger issues of Third World poverty, population growth, hunger, war, and revolution. For example, the countries of El Salvador, Honduras, and Nicaragua will double their populations in twenty-two years at present rates of growth. The labor force of these three countries alone will double between 1975 and 2000 to 13 million. Poverty, hunger, unemployment, and illiteracy remain serious problems, primarily as a result of an explosive growth in numbers far beyond the capacity of these nations. Add to this archaic political institutions, external ideological influences, and a poor natural resource base, and the ingredients for turmoil and civil conflict are abundant. As General Maxwell Taylor has warned, "If Central America today is an inviting pond to communist fishermen, under the conditions forecast it will offer them a well-stocked lake."

There is a vicious cycle of poor economic and political conditions in the Third World, and a consequent steady stream of migration to the United States. One may argue that present American immigration policy creates this vicious cycle through a lack of enforcement measures which then encourage and simplify Third World immigration to the United States.

Uncontrolled immigration may be undermining U.S. foreign policy in three further areas: (1) the inability of the United States to control its national borders directly weakens its national security; (2) the failure of the United States to adopt an enforceable immigration policy is leaving it open to international coercion; (3)

the traditional ability of the United States to provide a haven for victims of political oppression is impaired by the massive amount of illegal immigration, the majority seeking to improve their economic status, entering the country every year.

UNENFORCED BORDERS. It is often said that illegal immigration from the Third World acts as an important safety valve to relieve the population pressures there. Unfortunately, such a view obscures more important issues concerning U.S. national security. For example, while it is undeniably important that the United States maintain productive diplomatic relations with Mexico, in the words of the Economic Policy Council of the UNA-USA, one has to realize that "an unenforced border with Mexico is an unenforced border with the world."

Lacking enforceable immigration statutes, the United States faces pressure from the developing nations that will increase dramatically over the next two decades, just as it has over the past two. As migration increases, its ability to undermine the security of U.S. allies increases significantly as well. Already Somalia, Thailand, and Pakistan have been the recipients of massive movements of those fleeing civil war, political turmoil, and economic difficulty. Such refugee populations are seriously straining the civil and social order of these nations. Engendered as such problems are by the Soviet Union and others, it does not appear likely that these exoduses will be curtailed over the next generation. In fact, hostile countries will continue to find it convenient to expel dissidents and "bad" elements from their own societies, thereby at the same time creating further difficulties for their opposition.

INTERNATIONAL COERCION. The extent to which U.S. foreign and domestic policy can be manipulated by foreign governments, some openly hostile to U.S. interests, by the use of large-scale illegal immigrant flows, needs to be addressed. Because of its laxity with respect to enforcing the sovereignty of its own borders, the United States finds itself in a vulnerable position. How often will the United States, in the future, find itself reacting to the actions of a foreign power in a manner that is injurious to our society? Would countries threaten to cut off the flow of petroleum should the United States decide to enforce or strengthen its immigration statutes? Would Poland threaten to tighten the grip of martial law unless the United States agrees to accept a greater number of "Polish dissidents"? Would Vietnamese officials continue to exploit the desire of their own people to emigrate, bleeding them of precious life savings, because they know the United States would accept them, no questions asked? Does the United States accept whatever criminals the Cuban government deems it does not want simply because some among the group claim to be political refugees?

Will nations everywhere find in the United States a convenient refuge for its domestic dissidents or political opponents, thus eliminating a potential wellspring of political democracy? Does this country wish to continue to be met with threats from foreign governments wishing to get rid of people they find inconvenient? And how much leverage will this country have with other governments in efforts to have them accept their fair share of refugees and immigrants when they know that the United States itself has no effective means of controlling immigration?

REFUGEE POLICY. Refugees have become one of the more dominant trends in international migration. Along with the traditional element of political refugees have been added those people fleeing civil disturbance, wars, revolutions, coup d'etats, and generally poor economic conditions. Unfortunately, debate about refugee policy usually concerns domestic economic and political impacts with little discussion of the international considerations involved. U.S. refugee policy is in part a foreign policy issue; its importance will increase as the number of refugees in the world, almost 13 million in 1981, continues at present or higher levels.

Ambassador H. Eugene Douglas, U.S. coordinator for refugee affairs, has articulated the need to differentiate between immigrants, both legal and illegal, and refugees. He contends that it is essential that the United States establish a definition by which to determine who is a refugee, and therefore entitled to certain kinds of assistance, and who is an immigrant and therefore not entitled to refugee assistance. There lies a crucial distinction between refugees and immigrants, between the victims of political oppression and the victims or escapees from economic circumstances.

The foreign policy of the United States requires that this country be able to extend to those politically persecuted a safe haven.

This is a traditional and humanitarian aspect of U.S. policy, which most Americans associate with the best aspects of American society. In order to preserve this essential aspect, however, there is a need to maintain a foreign policy which has as one of its objectives, according to Douglas, "the protection of its frontiers from excessive illegal immigration." He argues further that the key is a policy which acknowledges the need for restricted entry while preserving the concept of refugee asylum.

## Conclusion

The national security of this nation depends upon its domestic strength and international stability. This strength requires an ability to control national borders, the maintenance of an independent foreign policy, a prosperous economy, and a cohesive domestic political environment. Uncontrolled migration is undermining this strength. Unchecked immigration, whatever its impact on labor and wage rates, does not just affect the unskilled and marginal job markets. Its impact, because of its sheer numbers and because of its illegality, affects the very fabric of American society, U.S. national security, cultural, political, and linguistic unity, economic well-being, and international standing.

The question is not whether a change in the foreign policy aspect of U.S. immigration will come but, rather, when and how it will come. There exist at least three possible scenarios: (1) the immigration policy status quo, slowly overwhelmed by events and forces that have already prompted cries of alarm, results in a radical policy departure in the form of total immigration restriction; (2) a laissez-faire approach to immigration problems results in fundamental alterations of U.S. society—a substratum of illegal aliens grows and an uneasy modus vivendi is found—and the United States is no longer a modern democracy but instead resembles the political order of the Greek city-state democracies; (3) between the extremes of one and two, a constructive response to the global immigration problem is found, resulting in a redirection of U.S. immigration policy as guided by a rational calculation of the national interest.

What is at issue is the need to discriminate among millions of potential immigrants, many equally deserving of consideration for entry into the United States. This implies a foreign policy agenda coupled with a difficult moral one. The demographic revolution of the past generation has delivered the most explosive growth in the labor force the world has seen to date. As this characteristic of the new immigration confronts this country, so must American policy responses be molded from a new appreciation of the times, of the changing global environment.

## SUPPLY-SIDE IMMIGRATION REFORM[4]

On June 20 [1983], speaking at a Republican Party dinner in Jackson, Mississippi, President Reagan warned that failure to increase U.S. military and economic aid to Central America would result in "a tidal wave of refugees—and this time they'll be 'feet people' and not 'boat people,' swarming into our country seeking a safe haven from communist repression to our south." Reagan was right in saying that there is a correlation between patterns of immigration and our economic and political policies at home and abroad. Unfortunately, the correlation he made was the wrong one.

Every thirty years or so the United States undergoes a xenophobic convulsion in the name of "immigration reform." The Simpson-Mazzoli Immigration Reform and Control Act, now before the House, is a product of the latest such spasm. Popular support for such "reform" is characteristically fanned by the sort of jingoism President Reagan resorted to in his Mississippi speech. In 1954, when hundreds of thousands of illegal Mexican workers were deported, the acting commissioner of the Immigration and Naturalization Service appealed to the gods of the cold war in testimony before Congress, saying that 100 "Communists and ex-Reds" were crossing the border daily. Today we are given dire

[4]Reprint of a magazine article by Geoffrey Rips, associate editor of *The Texas Observer*. *Nation*. 237:289+. O. 8, '83. Copyright © 1983 by Nation Magazine, The Nation Associates, Inc.

warnings of hordes of "feet people," and of the invasion of uncontrollable masses. "The swelling population of Mexico, driving millions of illegal aliens over the border," former Director of Central Intelligence William Colby said, "is a greater threat to the future of the United States than the Soviet Union."

Senator Alan Simpson of Wyoming, co-author of the immigration bill, has warned:

In the past several years a large majority of new legal immigrants joining American citizens and permanent residents in the United States has come from Latin America, Asia and the Caribbean area. With respect to illegal immigrants, it is estimated that Mexico is the source of at least 50 to 60 percent of the total, other parts of Latin America 10 to 15 percent, and the Caribbean area 5 to 10 percent. . . . If immigration continues at a high level, yet a substantial portion of these new persons and their descendants do not assimilate into the society, they have the potential to create in America a measure of the same social, political and economic problems from which they have chosen to depart. Furthermore, if language and cultural separatism rise above a certain level, the unity and political stability of the nation will—in time—be seriously diminished.

Allegedly to preserve the cultural integrity of this nation of immigrants from the consequences of a brown, black and yellow invasion, Senator Simpson and Representative Romano Mazzoli of Kentucky introduced a bill that would make it harder for refugees to receive political asylum and would tighten controls on immigration in a way calculated to encourage discriminatory hiring practices and union-busting by U.S. companies. The bill represents what National Immigration Coalition director Bert Corona calls "supply-side economics applied to the field of immigration." Moreover, as a means of stemming the influx, the bill would be ineffective.

That is because the proposed legislation does not address the peculiarities of the traffic across a border that was sparsely populated and largely undefined until the first part of this century. It does not take into account the reasons people leave their homelands for the United States. Most important, the Simpson-Mazzoli bill ignores the extent to which U.S. economic and political policies help create the patterns of immigration to the United States.

Any examination of immigration policy must consider both the "push" and the "pull" factors that cause people to migrate. In conventional analyses, these social forces are usually described as the pull of political freedom or economic opportunities and the push of repression or poverty. Only rarely is the government's role in manipulating those factors considered.

The McCarran-Walter Immigration and Nationality Act of 1952, for example, served as an important complement to cold war foreign policy. It was sponsored in the House by the chairman of the Un-American Activities Committee and contained an "ideological exclusion" clause and a "parole provision," which allowed the attorney general to admit or exclude any individual or group seeking political asylum.

The parole provision was first used to admit 34,000 Hungarian refugees in 1956. In the late 1950s and early 1960s, 650,000 Cubans were granted asylum under the provision and were given $994 million in immediate resettlement assistance by Congress. More than 130,000 South Vietnamese were permitted to settle in the United States during a two-year period in the mid-1970s, prior to the arrival of the Vietnamese "boat people." Most of them were members of the middle or upper class who had supported the Saigon government. Chileans who sought to enter the United States after Gen. Augusto Pinochet took power, in 1973, however, were not given blanket parole status; they were admitted on an individual basis. Edwin Ledbetter, speaking for the State Department in 1975, said, "This is really the first time since World War II we've made an effort to resettle people from a rightist regime. The determinations on security matters are more time-consuming." Secretary of State Henry Kissinger agreed that year to admit 400 selected Chilean refugees; two years later only 19 of them and their families were allowed to enter the United States.

Not only has the government been ideologically selective in who it allows to invade America's shores; it has also triggered large-scale migrations by its interventions in the affairs of other countries. Vietnam is an obvious example. U.S. support for the Duvalier regime in Haiti is another; through economic aid we have contributed to its longevity and the attendant repression. The

United States is, therefore, indirectly responsible for the boatloads of Haitians fleeing to Florida.

The U.S. hand is also evident in the emigration of large numbers of people from Central America to this country and Canada. Among those are Salvadorans fleeing the ravages of a war abetted by U.S. foreign aid. From 1980 to 1982, the United States gave $398 million in military aid and $275 million in economic aid to the Salvadoran government. Salvadorans are not emigrating because of their government's failure to subdue an armed opposition but because Washington is prolonging the war by shoring up a right-wing government, which refuses to allow its moderate and left-wing opponents to participate in elections and which perpetuates social inequities.

While the relationship between U.S. foreign and economic policy and the number of people seeking asylum here is obvious, the role the government plays in stimulating the flow of immigrant labor is no less significant. The history of Mexican labor in the southwestern United States is a history of the manipulation of these workers by U.S. agribusiness interests, aided by immigration legislation. To understand that history, we must begin at the nearly 2,000-mile border between Mexico and the United States. Throughout the nineteenth century, neither country made any effort to impede the flow of people back and forth across it, even after the present border was drawn up in 1848 in the Treaty of Guadalupe Hidalgo, ending the Mexican-American War. The flow was regulated by supply and demand, and the border's significance was largely a matter for cartographers. As Ernesto Galarzo, a farm-labor historian, wrote in *Merchants of Labor, the Mexican Bracero Story,* the Treaty of Guadalupe Hidalgo left "the toilers on one side of the border, the capital and best land on the other. This mistake immigration undertook to correct."

The demand for Mexican laborers rose markedly during World War I, and it was satisfied by poor Mexicans driven to seek work in the United States because the revolution of 1910 had left their country's economy in shambles. During the agricultural boom of the 1920s, the growers called for more Mexican workers, and the rate of border-crossings accelerated. Many of these immigrants found jobs in the fields owned by California's new agribusinesses.

In 1924, Congress passed the National Origins Act, which marked the beginning of a comprehensive Federal policy to control immigration through quotas. The act severely curtailed immigration from southern and Eastern Europe but set no quotas for immigrants from the countries of the Western hemisphere, who were needed to ease the resulting shortage of labor. That same year the Border Patrol was established to supervise the traffic of immigrants from below the Rio Grande.

In the 1930s, there was a backlash against Mexican workers because of widespread unemployment among Americans. The result was a crackdown on Mexican immigrant labor. Secretary of Labor William Doak declared, "One way to provide work for unemployed Americans is to oust any alien holding a job and to deport him." His words were followed by well-publicized raids by the Border Patrol and state and local police on farms employing Mexican workers. Many states started repatriation programs, under which several thousand Mexicans were shipped back to their homeland. Although those measures resulted in the deportation of only a small percentage of the Mexican workers in this country, the number of immigrants slowed to a trickle because of the scarcity of jobs. In 1934, President Lázaro Cárdenas implemented a long-promised agrarian reform program, which provided land to many Mexicans who might otherwise have sought work in the United States.

The growers in Southern California supported the government's efforts to deport Mexicans not only because they objected to their presence on already swollen relief rolls but also because they feared labor unrest. Seventy-five percent of the workers who participated in a series of strikes in 1933 by the Cannery and Agricultural Workers Industrial Union were from Mexico. Mexicans struck the melon growers of the Imperial Valley in 1928 and again in 1930, when 5,000 of them walked off the job. Local authorities arrested the organizers and deported them. The growers came to realize that while deportations did not significantly shrink the pool of Mexican labor, the threat of deportation did reduce protests about wages and working conditions and it made labor organizing more difficult.

The next great demand for Mexican labor came during World War II. The draft, along with the booming war economy, created a labor shortage and drove up farm workers' wages to levels that approached those in industry. Because the labor shortage was so acute, the Mexican government was able to win concessions protecting its citizens in the United States by working out a general migrant labor agreement, known as the bracero program. Under the terms of the agreement, Mexican workers received a guaranteed minimum wage and did not have to pay for their transportation. They could be used only in areas where there were labor shortages—not to depress wages or to break strikes. The Farm Security Administration acted as a contractor for the workers and enforced the terms of the program until it was transferred to the less stringent War Food Administration in 1943, following concerted lobbying by the growers.

In 1947 the agreement expired, but the growers convinced the two governments to extend the program under terms that allowed them to act as their own contractors. While that enabled them to get around some of the requirements of the program, many growers still felt constrained, and increasingly began to rely on undocumented workers, many of whom had first worked in the United States as braceros. A large number of those workers, who had been shipped home when their contracts expired, returned to the areas of their bracero employment, but this time as undocumented workers.

By 1951, the number of undocumented workers arrested by immigration police approached 500,000 (as compared with some 200,000 contract laborers admitted legally under the bracero program), and U.S. authorities attempted to establish greater control over the immigrant workers. This was accomplished in part by giving thousands of undocumented workers bracero contracts, usually with the same employers for whom they had been working illegally. In 1954 more than 300,000 Mexican workers were signed to contracts under the program. That same year the U.S. government initiated "Operation Wetback." One I.N.S. official claimed that "aliens who entered the United States illegally are responsible for 75 percent of all crimes committed in some Southern California and Texas counties. . . . Even more serious is the possibility that among the 'wetbacks' who seek employment there may be those whose entry would be detrimental to our national security." This operation, carried out in the name of the cold war, resulted in the deportation of more than 1 million undocumented laborers and produced a decline in the number of people apprehended by the I.N.S. while attempting to cross the border. Many workers joined the bracero program in Mexico rather than risk entering the United States illegally. In addition, by reducing the minimum contract period for braceros and by bypassing processing procedures set up by the Mexican government, the I.N.S. encouraged growers in the United States to comply with the system. As a result, the number of contract laborers rose to well over 400,000 during the late 1950s. The bracero program was terminated in 1964 because of opposition to mounting worker exploitation and increased lobbying by organized labor, and because Johnson Administration officials no longer saw the program as the solution to the problems caused by illegal immigration. The number of undocumented workers from Mexico apprehended in this country shot up to 100,000 in 1965, 350,000 in 1970 and more than 1 million in 1978.

While ostensibly set up to regulate the immigration of Mexicans to the United States, the bracero program had actually stimulated it. Through recruitment campaigns in Mexico during World War II, the program revived a migration process that had virtually ceased. And the work force mobilized by the program remained in this country illegally following its demise. Most of the employers in the United States who had relied on braceros for cheap labor continued to rely on these same workers, though their legal status had been terminated.

As the foregoing indicates, U.S. immigration policy has been, in the main, designed to benefit agriculture and industry in this country. It has provided them with a pool of cheap labor and has enabled the government to expel undesirable immigrants. Immigration policy created a pull that is partly responsible for the large immigrant work force in the United States today. The government's effort to curtail further immigration in 1964 by ending the bracero program was singularly unsuccessful, particularly in comparison with similar efforts in the early 1930s. That failure stemmed not from a diminished U.S. commitment to enforcing restrictive immigration policies but from the economic situation in Mexico. The termination of the bracero program coincided with the so-called Green Revolution in Mexico—a government project that financed irrigation systems for large corporate farms and encouraged an economy based on the international trade of commodities at the expense of local self-sufficiency. As a result, the operators of many small "rain-fed" farms were driven out of business, and small landholders and workers on communal farms, or *ejidos,* were forced to seek seasonal wage labor. By 1974, almost 5 million acres of rain-fed farmland had been abandoned. In the 1960s, the Mexican government began subsidizing urban industrial development. The products of the new industries in the cities replaced goods made by village artisans. That caused the decline of small local industries, an important source of income in rural areas, and set off a massive rural-to-urban migration. Many of the migrants left the land for the cities; when they could not find jobs in the cities, they crossed the border into the United States. Others were forced to supplement family incomes from subsistence farms and sought seasonal farm work in the United States. As Mexican economist Lourdes Arizpe points out, "All industrial nations recruit the bulk of their industrial work force from surplus agricultural labor." Arizpe calls rural-to-urban migration "the geographical expression of an economic process."

U.S. corporate interests gave added impetus to the forces in Mexico encouraging emigration. From 1950 to 1966, direct U.S. investment in Mexico increased from $286 million to almost $1.2 billion. Some jobs were created along the border by free-trade zones, which attracted American investment, and by the *maquiladores,* or runaway shops, designed to employ Mexican workers drawn to the border cities. In many cases these factories lured even more people from the hinterlands, who swelled the ranks of the urban unemployed. U.S. firms like Zenith, Motorola, Memorex, Burroughs and North American Rockwell opened plants in Mexico after receiving major concessions from the Mexican government. These concessions allowed them to exploit cheap Mexican labor and exempted them from certain export duties. This exacerbated balance of trade problems plaguing the Mexican economy.

Another example of the way U.S. policy has encouraged migration was pointed out by economist Michael Conroy, who wrote in *Socioeconomic Incentives for Migration from Mexico to the U.S.*:

The most significant determinant of substantially increased incentives for temporary migration from Mexico to the United States in recent years has been the devaluation of the peso relative to the dollar. . . . Policies of the World Bank and the International Monetary Fund, such as those imposed in 1976 for "stabilization" of the Mexican economy, are likely to contribute indirectly to the incentive for migration by slowing job creation while contributing directly through pressures for devaluation of the peso. If . . . the U.S. government backed and even encouraged such measures, U.S. policy has been significantly responsible for the increase in the incentive for temporary migration.

For the benefit of American investors abroad and American agribusiness and industry at home, a process was set in motion that has deposited the hordes on our doorstep.

The Immigration Reform and Control Act of 1983 is little more than an attempt to control those hordes. It would make it more difficult to gain political asylum and it would use the policing powers of the government to serve the needs of U.S. employers.

The xenophobic tenor of the campaign for the Simpson-Mazzoli legislation can be attributed to the desire of the bill's supporters to make undocumented laborers and political refugees scapegoats for the recent recession. But the charge that such workers take jobs away from Americans is open to dispute. In the recent recession, the areas of highest unemployment—the Midwest and the Northeast—did not suffer the largest influx of undocumented workers. Since the late 1970s, the Sun Belt has had the lowest rate of unemployment and has seen the largest influx of illegal immigrants.

Undocumented workers are frequently accused of putting a strain on social services. The truth is that they support a welfare system whose benefits they rarely see. The average stay in the United States for an undocumented worker from Mexico is two or three years, after which he returns to his family; thus he is not in this country long enough to collect many of the benefits for which his taxes have been deducted. According to studies conducted in the late 1970s by Jorge Bustamante of the Colegio de Mexico and by the U.S. Department of Labor, while taxes and Social Security were withheld from the paychecks of about 75 percent of undocumented workers, only 1.5 percent of all such individuals received food stamps, only 4 percent got unemployment compensation and only 4.5 percent had ever used public health services. Undocumented workers further subsidize the U.S. economy through the payment of sales tax. And the low wages most of them receive can be considered a form of subsidization of business.

Even if undocumented workers are not a drain on the economy, some organizations backing Simpson-Mazzoli, including the N.A.A.C.P., claim they depress wages and take jobs from American citizens and permanent residents. No doubt that is true on the fringes of the economy. But the answer, says Jim Harrington, an attorney for the Texas Civil Liberties Union, is not to "retaliate against people because they are hungry but to organize." The United Farm Workers of America, which opposes the Simpson-Mazzoli bill, has been working with labor groups in Mexico to organize farm workers.

The mechanisms proposed in the Simpson-Mazzoli bill for regulating immigrant labor include sanctions against employers, the "legalization" of various groups of undocumented workers, the implementation of a guest-worker program and the issuing of identification cards to all legal alien workers. The bill's supporters claim that sanctions would prevent employers from turning undocumented workers over to the I.N.S. after they have finished a job rather than paying them. The Mexican American Legal Defense and Educational Fund (MALDEF) argues that the penalties for hiring undocumented workers would not be a sufficient deterrent to prevent the practice. They may do little more than give employers an excuse to discriminate against members of certain ethnic groups even if they are permanent residents or citizens.

While the bill does not protect the right of undocumented workers to organize, it specifically includes unions that act as labor contractors among those against whom sanctions would apply. Unions place thousands of their members in jobs each year through hiring halls, and workers may join regardless of their legal status. The sanction provision would compel these unions to enforce the immigration laws, which would drive undocumented workers to nonunion contractors whose marginal operations leave them largely unaccountable to the government. This of course would eliminate the possibility of organizing a significant sector of the labor pool, which is one reason the American Federation of State, County and Municipal Employees, the International Longshoremen and Warehousemen's Union and the United Electrical Workers have spoken out against the Simpson-Mazzoli package. The A.F.L.-C.I.O., while calling for immigration reform, does not support the legislation passed by the Senate this summer [1983] and recommended by the House Judiciary Committee. Instead it favors the Hawkins-Miller amendment, which was proposed in the House Labor and Education Committee and which provides some protection for guest workers and a review mechanism for legalization decisions made by the I.N.S.

The "legalization" program proposed by the bill is purportedly intended to bring undocumented workers "out of the shadow," but instead it would legitimize a new subclass of workers. Under Mazzoli's H.R. 1510, all undocumented aliens who entered the country before 1982 would be eligible for amnesty and permanent resident status, while Simpson's S. 529 imposes a two-tiered system, with 1980 and 1982 as the cutoff years. Both proposals place the legalized workers in a legal limbo. Federal income tax and Social Security payments would be withheld from workers' paychecks, but they would not receive the full benefits. Legalized aliens would not be entitled to participate in federally funded assistance programs for a period of four years, although they would be entitled to emergency aid. According to MALDEF, the bill's imprecision in spelling out the social benefits and protections for which legalized workers are eligible presents an opportunity for exploitation. MALDEF also decries the fact that the bill does not specifically address the question of whether the families of legalized aliens would be allowed to enter the country and whether the workers would fall under the jurisdiction of the National Labor Relations Board, as they do under current law. If 1980 is used as the cutoff for determining which aliens receive permanent resident status, more than half of the undocumented workers in the United States today would not qualify, since, as mentioned, most stay no longer than two or three years. Many of those would be eligible for temporary resident status. However, under both versions of the bill all undocumented workers must be screened for eligibility by immigration officials, whose criteria will include the ideological exclusion clause of the McCarran-Walter Act.

The ID system is intended to keep track of all alien workers, who would be registered with the I.N.S. and whose records would be maintained on a computerized index. Guest workers, whose stay in the United States would be specifically limited by the requirements of a particular job, would be drawn from lists of available workers compiled by the Mexican government. The U.S. government would contract for the guest workers with employers, and they would not be covered by any union contracts in force where they work. Neither bill proposes mechanisms to safeguard the rights of guest workers. Moreover, the Panetta amendment to the bill, which has been passed by the House Agriculture Committee, does away with the requirement that employers certify the unavailability of American workers before applying for guest workers to harvest perishable crops. The guest-worker plan is little more than a government-supervised program that would enable employers to hire cheap labor and free them from having to make contributions to Social Security and unemployment compensation funds.

The Simpson-Mazzoli guest-worker plan is essentially an expansion of the current H-2 program, instituted in 1952 to fill temporary jobs with foreign workers if unemployed Americans are not available. Under that program wage standards are set by the U.S. Department of Labor, and employers can control which workers are hired. In 1976, H-2 melon pickers in Presidio, Texas, struck, demanding the pay the government had guaranteed. The strike was eventually settled, but the following year none of the strikers were rehired. When the U.F.W. began to organize farm laborers in northern Mexico before they came to the United States, growers under the H-2 program started to fly in workers from southern Mexico and Guatemala.

Political refugees fare no better than immigrant workers under the Simpson-Mazzoli bill. The bill calls for the summary deportation of aliens who enter without documents unless they assert some "reasonable basis" for legal entry or apply for asylum within fourteen days after the issuance of an order to show cause why they should not be deported. An alien who misses the deadline will not be allowed to apply for political asylum unless there is a change in his home government that might affect his eligibility. The bill reduces the time for appealing a deportation order from six months to thirty days.

Those provisions are designed to streamline the procedures for handling political asylum requests. Since most refugees will not be able to ascertain their rights and the steps they must take to receive asylum within the first two weeks of entry (when most arrests occur), much less find a lawyer who can prepare the necessary papers within that time, the political asylum provisions of the bill amount to little more than a mechanism to allow the summary deportation of large numbers of aliens. This would relieve the crowded conditions at detention centers in Florida, Texas and California, but it is not in keeping with the right to due process afforded all who come under the jurisdiction of the U.S. government, and it violates human rights conventions to which the United States is a signatory. While the House bill provides for judicial review of decisions on asylum, exclusion and deportation cases, the original Senate bill did not. Before it passed the full Senate, Edward Kennedy attached an amendment providing for such review. Those seeking judicial review would, of course, need a certain amount of knowledge about U.S. courts as well as money to pay for counsel.

After the Senate passed S. 529, it was expected that Mazzoli's bill would move through the House in a similar fashion. But several committees took an interest in it, which slowed its progress, as has President Reagan's recent courtship of Hispanic voters. In addition, talk of economic recovery has made the legislation seem less urgent to many members of Congress. It is now scheduled for consideration by the House Rules Committee on October 18.*

Even if the bill is passed, it cannot solve the problems it claims to address. Real immigration reform will come only through an understanding of the economic and political factors that create mass migrations. As long as the United States is willing to exploit

---

*After several delays, the bill was approved by the House in June of 1984.

cheap immigrant labor and tolerate the economic imbalance that exists between the First World and the Third World, as long as it supplies arms to other nations and exacerbates conflict in other parts of the world, it will always have an "immigration problem."

---

## DON'T CLOSE OUR BORDERS[5]

---

Many Americans think of immigrants as the tired and poor. And too many believe that they live on welfare or that they displace natives from scarce jobs by accepting low wages. These complaints and others will be heard as Congress tries to secure this country's borders by way of the Simpson-Mazzoli bill. The proposed law includes amnesty for longtime illegal immigrants, sanctions against those who hire them and a national identity card, but its main impact would be to reduce the total number of illegal and legal immigrants into the United States.

Opponents of immigration believe they are guarding their own economic interests when they argue that immigrants damage our pocketbooks and our environment. But recent research shows that many of their beliefs are dead wrong and are based on myth.

• **Myth 1.** *The United States is being flooded by Mexican illegals.* Leonard Chapman, then the commissioner of the Immigration and Naturalization Service, first scared us in the 1970s with an estimate that up to 12 million people were illegally in this country. It was just a guess, but now ingenious statisticians using a variety of methods report that the total number of illegals is almost certainly below 6 million, and may be only 3.5 to 5 million. Furthermore, the number of illegals in the country overstates the number of Mexicans who intend to remain permanently, leaving perhaps 1.3 million Mexican illegals—certainly not a large number by any economic test, and far less than the scare figures promulgated earlier.

• **Myth 2.** *Illegal and legal immigrants abuse welfare and govern-*

[5]Reprint of a column by sociologist Julian L. Simon. *Newsweek* 103:11. F. 27, '84. Copyright © 1984 by Newsweek, Inc. All rights reserved. Reprinted by permission.

*ment services.* Study after study shows that small proportions of illegals use government services: free medical, 5 percent; unemployment insurance, 4; food stamps, 1; welfare payments, 1; child schooling, 4. Illegals are afraid of being caught if they apply for welfare. Practically none receive social security, the costliest service of all, but 77 percent pay social-security taxes, and 73 percent have federal taxes withheld.

In an analysis of Census Bureau data I conducted for the Select Commission on Immigration and Refugee Policy, I found that, aside from social security and Medicare, immigrant families average about the same level of welfare services as do citizens. When programs for the elderly are included, immigrant families use far *less* public funds than do natives. During the first five years in the United States, the average immigrant family receives $1,404 (in 1975 dollars) in welfare compared with $2,279 received by a native family. The receipts become equal in later years, but when immigrants retire, their own children contribute to their support and so they place no new or delayed burdens upon the tax system.

Immigrants also pay more than their share of taxes. Within three to five years, immigrant-family earnings reach and pass those of the average American family. The tax and welfare data together indicate that, on balance, immigrants contribute to the public coffers an average of $1,300 or more each year that family is in the United States.

• **Myth 3.** *Immigration is high.* An article in the prestigious journal Foreign Affairs states that "immigration and refugee flows to the United States in the late 1970s were at or near the highest levels ever experienced." This is just wrong even in absolute terms. There were 800,000 immigrants in 1980—the most recent high— yet near the turn of the century and for six years, immigration topped the million mark. The burden of absorbing it was, in fact, greater then. Between 1901 and 1910, immigrants constituted 9.6 percent of the population: between 1961 and 1970, they were only 1.6 percent. Or consider this. In 1910, 14.6 percent of the population was foreign-born. In 1970 only 4.7 percent had been born abroad, or less than 1 person in 20, including those who had come many years ago. Amazingly, this "country of immigrants," as the politicians often put it, has a smaller share of foreign-borns than more "homogeneous" countries like Great Britain, Sweden, Switzerland, France, Australia and Canada.

• **Myth 4.** *Immigrants are "huddled masses"—uneducated and unskilled.* The central economic fact now—as it has been throughout U.S. history—is that, in contrast to the rapidly aging U.S. population, immigrants tend to arrive in their 20s and 30s, when they are physically and mentally vigorous and in the prime of their work life. On average, they have about as much education as do natives, and did so even at the turn of the century. Immigrants also tend to be unusually self-reliant and innovative; they have the courage and the belief in themselves that is necessary for the awesome challenge of changing one's culture and language.

• **Myth 5.** *Immigrants cause native unemployment.* This has always been the major fear. If the number of jobs is fixed and immigrants occupy some jobs, then there are fewer jobs for natives. This overlooks the dynamic that immigrants create jobs as well as take them. Their purchases increase the demand for labor, leading to new hires. They frequently open small businesses that are a main source of new jobs.

Experiments conducted by INS show little, if any, damage to citizens even in the few areas where immigrants—legal and illegal—concentrate: in the restaurant and hotel industries. Most Americans, having better alternatives (including welfare programs), do not accept these jobs on the conditions offered.

On balance, immigrants are far from a drag on the economy. As workers, consumers, entrepreneurs and taxpayers, they invigorate it and contribute healthy economic benefits. By increasing the work-force, they also help solve our social-security problem. Immigrants tend to come at the start of their work lives but when they retire and collect social security, they typically have raised children who are then contributing taxes to the system.

This country needs more, not fewer, immigrants. The U.S. birthrate is low and our future work force is shrinking. By opening our doors we will not only do good but the evidence indicates we will also do well.

# V. A WORLD PROBLEM

## EDITOR'S INTRODUCTION

The United States is by no means the only nation beset by large numbers of immigrants. Pakistan, for example, accepted almost 3 million Afghan refugees after the Soviet invasion of Afghanistan in 1980. Few will return; they are immigrants in all but name, straining Pakistan's weak economy and creating a ripple effect in the world economy by forcing thousands of Pakistanis to seek work in the industrial centers of Europe and the Middle East. Violent outbreaks of xenophobia triggered by the entry of incompatible immigrants are also on the rise in many parts of the world. One of the worst of these occurred in India in 1983, when Hindu Assamese, protesting the presence of millions of Muslims from neighboring Bangladesh, slaughtered some 360 Bangladeshis.

The understanding of international migrations is crucial to the management of the world economy, but the control of mass movements of peoples would require a level of international cooperation never before achieved. The need for international reform is pressing. "Negotiating rules of conduct will be difficult, and success will be slow in coming," writes Jagdesh Bhagwati, an expert on the international economy, "but the task is urgent and compelling."

The first selection in this section describes the unforeseen results of Western Europe's "guestworker" programs of the 1960s and '70s—resentment and prejudice by Europeans against some 12 million alien laborers who are there to stay. Nigeria's abrupt expulsion of its unemployed immigrants in 1983 is discussed in the second selection, an article by Val Ross for *Maclean's*. Ross predicts that the deportation of masses of economic refugees may become common in the future. In the last selection, Leon F. Bouvier provides a summary of recent global immigrations. He cites the economic imbalance between North and South and the rapid growth of the labor force of the poorer nations as causing record levels of migration. "Conflict and suffering are inevitable," Bouvier writes, "but we must do what we can to hold them to a minimum."

---

## RISING RACISM ON THE CONTINENT[1]

---

*Yesterday the Jews, tomorrow the Turks.*

—Graffito in West Berlin

*"We don't want to resort to extremism, but if we are pushed against the wall, we will defend ourselves."*

—A young Moroccan in Paris

*Urgent action is needed if [racial disadvantage] is not to become an endemic, ineradicable disease threatening the very survival of our society.*

—Lord Scarman's report on the 1981 riots in Brixton, England

They came by the millions when times were good, from backward villages in Anatolia and the Punjab, from the Caribbean and North Africa. For the most part, they were welcome, even sought after. They constituted a willing and indispensable *Lumpenproletariat* for Western Europe's postwar boom, ready to do work no one else wanted to do. Their large families, their mosques, their exotic costumes and customs were merely transitory inconveniences. One day they would vanish: the "migrants," the *gastarbeiters,* the *travailleurs immigrés* would simply go home. But they stayed, and a new generation grew to adulthood: dark-skinned youngsters sporting the accents of Provence, Bavaria or

[1]Reprint of a magazine article by John Nielsen and *Time* staff reporters. *Time.* 123:40+. F. 6, '84.

the Midlands. Willy-nilly, the societies of Western Europe had become multiracial.

The transformation was largely complete by the mid-'70s. But by then, under the twin prods of hard times and rising unemployment, the immigrant question had become a political issue. Responding to pressure from their voters, governments placed heavy restrictions on new immigration. Too late. A new alien and highly visible population was already entrenched in ghettos across the Continent: in Kreuzberg, along the Wall, in West Berlin; in large areas of Paris, Marseilles, Lyons; in the old quarters of Amsterdam and Utrecht; in the Brussels communes of Saint-Josse, Saint-Gilles and Schaerbeek; in Brixton, Toxteth and two dozen other working-class communities around Britain.

All told, an estimated 12 million immigrants from less-developed countries live in Western Europe, many of them trapped between old countries that cannot feed them and new countries that no longer want them.

As the Continent's recession has dragged on, many West Europeans have begun looking for scapegoats and have found them among their minorities. Suddenly the Turks, Pakistanis and Algerians are no longer individuals: they are *Kanaken,* nig-nogs and *bougnouls.* Occasionally the prejudice goes from verbal violence to physical: a gang attack, an anonymous bullet, a bomb thrown from a passing car. More often racism comes at arm's length: random insults, hostile stares, racial stereotypes held up as universal truths. "Yes, I suppose I'm prejudiced," says a West London matron. "People my age had nothing to do with the blunders and greed of the upper classes toward the colonies, and I don't see why I should put up with the results now. The first thing the blacks do is go on welfare. And I'm tired of people working in the post office who don't speak proper English."

Inevitably, the animosity has found political echoes. France's far-right Front National probably commands no more than 3% support nationwide, but it has made significant electoral gains in some communities with large immigrant populations. The Netherlands' ultraconservative Centrum-Partij, playing the racial theme to the hilt, finds similar support. In Britain and West Germany, right-wingers in the ruling parties have thundered ominously about racial issues, to the embarrassment of their colleagues.

In a sense, the political rumblings represent a mulish refusal to accept the changes in Western Europe's social fabric. Serious debate has been hindered by rhetoric about immigration, which is all but over, and large-scale repatriation, which is all but impossible. "We haven't come to terms with the fact that black people are really here to stay," says lawyer Paul Boateng, 32, who was an unsuccessful Labor candidate in Britain's last general election. "We regard black people as immigrants who are transients, or potentially transients. White society wants to believe it's all a bad dream—that they will wake up one morning and all the blacks will be gone. Well, it's not going to happen."

Even in the good years, Western Europe exploited and ignored its minorities, but the long-running recession seems to have stirred a particularly malignant demon in the Continent's psyche. In France last month, a dispute over extensive layoffs at a Peugeot factory outside Paris degenerated into three days of racial violence that left 120 people injured. The clashes pitted striking workers (mostly immigrants) against those still holding jobs (mostly Frenchmen). More than 20 immigrants have been killed or wounded in other incidents in France in the past year. At least seven, including a ten-year-old boy, were victims of snipers in the tense, ethnically mixed housing complexes outside Paris and other major cities. Racist harassment in Britain is so common that nonwhites no longer bother to report threats, insults or obscene letters to the police. In 1981 the Home Office found that West Indians were 36 times more likely to be racially attacked than whites, Asians 50 times.

The violence has chilling resonance in West Germany, where small neo-Nazi groups have seized the race issue and made it their own. Turkish immigrants regularly receive threatening letters telling them to leave Germany or be hounded out. An outfit calling itself the Prince Eugen Battle Group (named for a brutal Austrian field marshal who led a major assault against the Turks in the late 17th century) has set its sights on Turkish teachers in West Berlin schools. "Can't you understand we [Germans] don't want anything to do with you," says one of their milder letters. "Pack your things while there is still time . . . before your apartments and kebab stalls go up in flames." All too often, the threats are carried out. In West Berlin, a group of teen-age German thugs, screaming abuse at foreigners, attacked a Turkish shop last November, roughing up the owner and his family and ransacking the rooms. In Heidelberg, scores of right-wing fanatics assaulted migrant workers and paraded through the city shouting neo-Nazi slogans. Police arrested 25.

Football and bigotry seem to go hand in hand among some West German youth gangs. Fans for Dortmund's Borussia soccer team regularly sing Nazi songs and chant *Heil, Hitler!* in the stands and terrorize immigrants after matches. At present, 37 members of the group are being investigated on charges of racial incitement, theft, assault and breach of the peace. When West Germany played Turkey last November in a qualifying match for this year's European championships, police posted 6,000 men at West Berlin's Olympic stadium. Turkish shops were given special protection after neo-Nazi groups threatened that the Kreuzberg ghetto would "go up in flames" on the day of the game. The anti-immigrant atmosphere caused Chancellor Helmut Kohl so much embarrassment that he flew in from Bonn to attend the game.

Not long ago, Tara Mukherjee's job as a manager with a British mutual fund took him to Belgium. Although born in India, Mukherjee, 54, has lived in Britain for 35 years, and is permitted to enter and leave the country freely. As he was departing this time, an immigration official quizzed him closely about his new passport, apparently looking for grounds to detain him as a suspected illegal. To the official's embarrassment, Mukherjee's documents were in order. "I watched his face redden as he stamped my passport," Mukherjee remembers. It was an example of what he calls "lace-curtain discrimination. It's where you discriminate in subtle ways without being detected. It's in all walks of British life."

The curtain, of course, is by no means solely British. Customs officials around the Continent routinely single out dark-skinned travelers for special scrutiny. Taxi drivers in the Dutch city of Nijmegen refused to accept black customers after one Surinamese failed to pay his fare. Brussels abounds with signs that say FOR RENT with a NO FOREIGNERS footnote. The message, which is illegal, normally does not apply to Europeans. The owner of a sidewalk café on West Berlin's Kurfiirstendam excludes Turks because they "lower the tone" of his establishment. Says Brahim Chanchabi, 29, a Tunisian student in Paris: "You see it in people's eyes. It's not so much a look of hatred as of fear. The other day an elderly woman just started yelling at me, saying 'Go back to your own country!'"

Mass migration is nothing new in European history. The Continent's religious, dynastic and economic upheavals have uprooted people for centuries: Eastern Jews to the West, French Huguenots to Germany, and most recently, Spaniards, Portuguese and Italians to the factories of the north. Every wave of émigrés has met resistance.

Today's non-European immigrants come from alien cultures: some are descended from Islamic ancestors who struggled to the death with Christendom, while others bear the brunt of attitudes hardened by a long history of colonialism. "There is a notion of racial superiority in Britain, and it relates to the myth of empire," says Malcolm Cross, deputy director of the Research Unit on Ethnic Relations at Birmingham's Aston University. "The empire was a reality. In 1939 this country controlled a quarter of the world's population. But the myth was based on a spurious notion of racial superiority." With some minor adjustments for fact, the statement can be applied to Western Europe as a whole.

There are other tenets in the anti-immigrant canon, and like the myth of white supremacy, they do not stand up to close examination. For example, that immigrants take jobs from local citizens. Although there is some competition for low-paying jobs, there is no correlation between unemployment rates and immigrant populations. A West German Labor Ministry official insists that largely due to unemployment and mechanization, Germans are more and more attracted to jobs they once considered too menial, like garbage collecting. But a recent study by the city of Düsseldorf showed that it would grind to a virtual halt if the foreigners withdrew their labor. Garbage would remain stinking on sidewalks, hospitals would not be able to cope, and there would be some closure of schools. In addition, the city would lose $3.6 million in taxes and $6.1 million in pension contributions. Says French Sociologist Jacqueline Costa-Lascoux: "The attempt to substitute a national labor force for immigrant labor has largely been a failure. Even in times of economic crisis and unemployment, there are certain jobs that nationals will just not take." Official studies show that "fewer than three foreign workers in ten could be replaced by French workers."

Sometimes the newcomers' rage boils over, as it did in Brixton, Liverpool and Lyons in the long, hot summer of '81. More often it is sublimated into sadness, disillusionment and steely resentment, or it sinks back into the ineffable apathy that seems the most common defense against a harsh life. In Britain, the unemployment rate among blacks is twice that of whites; similarly, joblessness among immigrant Turks in West Germany is twice that of native Germans; among immigrants in France, it is one quarter higher than for native French.

The prospect of long-term idleness is roughest on young immigrants, as it is for all youngsters, blighting their lives when they should be taking wing. The hopelessness can sink deep roots. Young blacks in Britain point to their unemployed elders and ask why they should even bother to try to find jobs. "How long does a person go on knocking on the door?" asks Aaron Haynes, a black sociologist and director of community affairs for Britain's Commission for Racial Equality. "Unless there is some degree of success, you are just adding one more round to the syndrome of failure—and that's what the black community is suffering from at the moment."

Drug abuse, prostitution and assorted other crimes—minor and major—flourish in many immigrant ghettos. Young Turks and Surinamese are deeply involved in the narcotics trade around Amsterdam; addiction is common among young North Africans in Paris. Says Nordine Iznasni, 21, a resident of the notorious Cité Gutenberg, a collection of ramshackle, barrack-like buildings in the Paris suburb of Nanterre: "When you've got nothing to do and nothing to look forward to, it's a way to hide from reality, just as French kids do. Young North Africans are sick of rejection, unemployment and disrespect. Unless you have a strong character, it's easy to fall into." Studies by France's Social Affairs and Solidarity Ministry indicate, however, that immigrants are no more delinquent than native Frenchmen of equivalent age and social situation.

There are, of course, many Europeans committed to promoting racial understanding. Some have even begun to redirect national policies. France's Socialist government has cracked down heavily on illegal immigration, but it has also given priority to job training and housing programs for minorities. To ease the pain of the Peugeot layoffs, for instance, authorities are considering a program of retraining for workers who choose to stay in France and payments—perhaps as much as $4,700 each—to those who choose repatriation. Britain's Conservative government, whose anti-immigration policies have been denounced as "oppressive" by its Labor Party opponents, is trying to head off a repeat of the 1981 Brixton riots. Police have abandoned some of the antagonistic practices of the past and have moved to establish better community relations, and modest amounts of money have been earmarked for the most blighted urban areas. The mayor of West Berlin has appointed a commissioner for German-Turkish relations. In The Netherlands, the Anne Frank Foundation (established in 1957 to save the house where the young Jewish fugitive wrote her famous diary) supplies 2,500 schools with antiracist study materials.

Experts in both countries are studying the American experience in coping with ethnic strains. "The U.S. model is important because the country has traditionally had a large immigrant population," says Georgina Dufoix, France's Secretary of State for Families and Immigrants. "One thing that has interested me most is the effort to see that there are always blacks in [responsible positions] in order to give the black population an image of itself and its role in American society." Says Britain's Boateng: "America still has deep-rooted racism, but at least there has been a recognition of that fact and a political will to do something about it. Here society as a whole doesn't recognize racism, and there's no political will or machinery to change it."

Meanwhile, a number of time bombs are ticking. Racial tensions are palpable in the big cities of Britain and France; both countries, and some others as well, are worried about possible ex-

plosions. Says Zafir Ilgar, 35, the leader of the Turkish community in West Berlin: "Bonn must recognize that we Turks are here
to stay. The whole climate is one of fear and unease. The careless
speeches of some politicians are causing Germans to direct their
aggression against foreign workers." The strains will not go away
by themselves. In Britain, 45% of ethnic minorities were actually
born there. In Brussels, foreigners will make up 40% of the population by the year 2000. In a recent report on immigrant youth,
French Government Demographers James Marange and André
Lebon predicted that within 15 years, more than half of those under 25 in France will be of foreign origin.

Many of them, moreover, will be citizens, voters with the potential ability to swing elections. Second-generation immigrants
are beginning to grasp that possibility, and they too are drawing
a lesson from the U.S. "The Americans brought slaves from Africa; the French brought our parents here from Algeria, weak and
ignorant, just like blacks," says one young man in the Cité Gutenberg. "If we start to think, improve ourselves and make demands,
it could lead to something like this . . . " As he speaks, he ges-
tures toward a photograph of Jesse Jackson, then finishes his sen-
tence, " . . . to political power."

## AN EXODUS OF THE UNWELCOME[2]

To the shoving, burdened, half-starved mob it was at best a
bittersweet reception. WELCOME TO GHANA proclaimed the hastily
designed bulletin board just inside the Ghanaian-Togo border at
Aflao. Refugees from Nigeria's crumbling economy and internal
politics, hundreds of thousands of non-Nigerians were victims of
the Lagos government's Jan. 17 edict: by Jan. 31 all illegal, unemployed and unskilled foreign workers had to leave the country.
The order prompted the largest migration on the continent since
the mid-1800s. Club-wielding police drove the refugees onto cattle

[2]Reprint of an article by Val Ross and Maclean's staff reporters. Maclean's. 96:20–1. F. 14, '83. Copyright © 1983 by Maclean Hunter. All rights reserved. Reprinted by permission.

cars, ships, buses, trucks, taxis, dugout canoes and motorcycles. Some even fled on foot, clutching remnants of their existence in black Africa's richest nation: mattresses, string bags of canned goods and cheap stereo cassette players. All of them shared a private history of broken dreams.

Ghanaian nationals were by far the largest single group to flee Nigeria. But the miserable tide of roughly 1.5 million jobless and homeless deportees washed across all of West Africa. In Togo, trucking ground to a halt as the country's fleet was requisitioned to ferry the refugees. Nations as far-flung as Senegal and Upper Volta rapidly constructed reception centres. But as the destitute countries reeled under the sudden burden of hundreds of thousands of returning citizens, the refugees themselves faced an equally grim reality: there were fewer jobs in their homelands than when they had left to be part of Nigeria's oil dream.

The unfolding West African tragedy once again highlighted the vulnerability of the world's estimated 25 million "guest workers." They work legally or without official papers in countries where they are tolerated only because they are prepared to work in jobs that citizens will not accept. They are discriminated against, usually underpaid (the Soviet Union's 11,000 Vietnamese guest workers earn as little as $5 a month), and they are the first to suffer when their host countries' unemployment rates begin to rise. Still, no member nation has accepted the International Labour Organization's formal recommendation that migrant workers should have the right to appeal an expulsion order.

Last week, as oil prices weakened, three million guest workers in the Gulf states, one million in Venezuela, and even foreign workers in the tiny oil-producing African nation of Gabon, also feared for their jobs. Gabon's 25,000 French nationals, most of them linked with the oil industry, have already been threatened with mass expulsion for opposing the country's new links with U.S. oil companies. But for the guest workers of Nigeria, whose oil markets have virtually dried up, the issue was already settled. A $4-billion drop in oil revenues and an unemployment rate of almost 25 percent had stirred public discontent with Prime Minister Shehu Shagari's government, which faces a general election in six months. As an expelled foreign worker, Stephen Antwi, remarked bitterly: "We have seen the devil, and he is a Nigerian politician anxious to win an election."

Compounding the brutal two-week timetable given to Nigeria's guest workers was the fact that few of them could afford the exorbitant plane fare home. As many as 100,000 camped for a week on the open docks of Lagos port waiting for boats, then, literally clinging to portholes and rigging as the boats departed, they made the 15-hour trip to Accra.

For days, travelling by grossly overloaded boat seemed the refugees' only option. Overland routes were inaccessible because the intervening border between Togo and Ghana had been closed since Sept. 21 as part of a regional dispute. But the flood of refugees to transit camps strung across the 190-km route from Nigeria through Benin and Togo to the closed border at Aflao quickly overwhelmed their holding capacity. Diplomatic pressure mounted on Ghana to reach an agreement with Togo. Then, on Jan. 28, Togo's president, Gen. Gnassingbe Eyadéma, summoned Ghana's minister of the interior, Johnny Hansen, to the Togolese capital. After a stormy argument, the two men drove to the Benin-Togo border at Sanvee-Kondji, where the Ghanaian saw thousands of refugees huddled between the border posts, starving and shivering in the chill night. He immediately fired off a Telex to his superiors in Accra. The government relented; on Jan. 29 it opened the border crossing point for 12 hours and, two days later, agreed to keep it open around the clock.

Meanwhile the creaking machinery of international aid rumbled into action. Last week the European Community sent $6 million to help feed the deportees; Canada has preliminarily earmarked $100,000, and last Saturday officials of the UN Disaster Relief Office (UNDRO) arrived in Accra to co-ordinate UN efforts. But the refugees themselves credited gifts of bread, bananas and water from private citizens of Togo and Benin for their survival. Among them was Kwame Asamoadu, who told *Maclean's* that the exodus had been particularly painful for him and his wife. "She was nine months pregnant, but we had no choice," he said. Asamoadu's wife gave birth at the Ghanaian border. But both mother and child are healthy. "God is wonderful," Asamoadu rejoiced. Indeed, the expulsion was remarkably free of disaster.

To justify the expulsions, the Lagos government argued that the guest workers had been responsible for a rising crime rate and for religious riots which resulted in at least 4,000 deaths in 1981 and hundreds more last October. In fact the few aliens implicated in those riots were not Ghanaian, but Moslem fundamentalists from Cameroon. Still, most African nations muted their criticism of Nigeria's arbitrary move. But in the long run, the country's spasm of xenophobia may undercut the credibility of its promotion of regional economic co-operation. Said Julius Ihonvbere, an African trade specialist now studying at the University of Toronto: "As others see that Nigeria's promises, and its commitment to joint projects in the region, are at the mercy of North Sea oil prices, they will begin to look for other allies." For the rest of West Africa, the eventual impact could be even more destructive. Upper Volta has lost the contributions that its citizens working abroad used to send to their destitute homeland—payments that equal as much as 60 per cent of its export earnings. In Ghana the military government of Flt. Lt. Jerry Rawlings faces the awesome prospect of trying to reintegrate the deportees into the country's moribund agricultural sector. The country's political system, rocked by the coup that brought Rawlings to power in late 1981 and further shaken by a second unsuccessful coup attempt last November, remains an open question. Its population has grown by almost five per cent in two weeks.

As the dust of the exodus began to settle, the global issue of guest workers remained. Despite the hardship endured by the refugees, an internationally recognized code protecting guest workers remains a distant dream. Western nations, grappling with double-digit unemployment figures, are becoming increasingly heavy-handed with their immigrant workers. Ottawa is currently considering putting its estimated 200,000 illegal aliens on six years' probation rather than carrying out its original intention to grant them an amnesty. In the future, the world's roads are likely to become choked at any time with people whose cheap labor is no longer an asset.

# HUMAN WAVES[3]

When the problem of worldwide population growth is mentioned, attention is almost always focused on fertility rates. Yet another side of the population problem is causing mounting concern—the movement across national borders of millions of people in search of a better life. People have always dreamed of moving to greener pastures, but never in recorded history have migration levels approached those of today. The rising tide of migrants is raising legal and ethical questions that nations have not previously had to face.

Some thirty-five years ago, American sociologist-demographer Kingsley Davis wrote:

Not only is the earth's total population increasing at the fastest rate ever known, but the increase is extremely unequal as between different regions. Generally the fastest growth is occurring in the poorest regions: the slowest growth in the richest. . . . Between the two kinds of areas the differences in level of living are fantastic. What is more natural than to expect the destitute masses of the underprivileged regions to swarm across international and continental boundaries into the better regions? . . . One wonders how long the inequities of growth between major regions can continue without an explosion that will somehow quickly restore the imbalance.

Davis's prediction is beginning to be realized. People do not move simply because they are crowded; they move because there is not enough food, jobs are scarce, and wages are low in their home countries. If population growth levels had been falling instead of rising during the 1950s and 1960s, conditions would be far less difficult in most countries. Unfortunately, nothing can be done about past demographic behavior. We are just now beginning to witness the impact of the decline in mortality that occurred during the 1950s and 1960s, particularly infant and child mortality, while fertility remained high. Those fifties and sixties babies are now entering adulthood, moving to cities, and forming their

[3]Reprint of a magazine article by Leon F. Bouvier, senior research associate at the Population Reference Bureau, Washington, D.C. With permission from *Natural History*, Vol. 92, No. 8 (Ap '83). Copyright © the American Museum of Natural History, 1983.

own households and families. That is why, in Mexico, for example, despite the decline in fertility among individual women, the country's current population of 75 million will surpass 175 million in less than fifty years. There, and in many other less developed countries, the sheer numbers of women entering reproductive age will keep the overall rate of natural increase high. So while we must reinforce our efforts to lower fertility, that will not solve the problem of millions upon millions of young adults seeking a better way of life now.

For years, many demographers saw the 3 percent rates of growth—meaning a doubling of the population in less than twenty-five years—as problems only for underdeveloped nations. We expressed the opinion that such unprecedented growth could not continue for very long—death rates would soon climb as a rapidly growing population encountered a dwindling supply of resources. But now that the beneficiaries of declining infant and child mortality have come of age, the true impact of the population explosions in the developing countries is being felt not only in those countries but also in the advanced countries, as immigration levels swell.

In 1940, 65 percent of the people on the earth lived in developing countries; today the number approaches 75 percent of the 4.6 billion world population. In a short seventeen years it will surpass 80 percent of some 6.1 billion people. Increasingly, residents of the poorest nations are making the decision to move across international borders in an attempt to improve their lives. But with the emergence of nation-states and political barriers, migration has become subject to control. To people facing the prospect of staggering poverty at home, the spectacular advances in communications and transportation have made the possibly dire consequences of migration seem less risky than staying put. This is becoming evident all over the planet as people move from Mexico and Central America to the United States; from Guinea to the Ivory Coast; from Colombia to Venezuela; even from such small islands as Saint Vincent and Saint Lucia to Barbados. Some are legal migrants whose decision to move results from considerable discussion and thought; some 13 million are refugees forced to abandon their homelands for political reasons; some are illegal migrants who enter a country surreptitiously and lead guarded lives for fear of apprehension. The effects of these movements across borders are awesome and differ substantially from one region to another.

When Third World countries exhibit rapid industrial growth, as some OPEC nations have in recent years, they attract residents from less fortunate neighboring states. Thus in Kuwait and the United Arab Emirates, 75 to 80 percent of the population are immigrants—temporary residents who are not citizens and in all likelihood will never become citizens. Illegal immigrants from such impoverished countries as Colombia and Ghana have swarmed to Venezuela and Nigeria. The recent forced exodus of Ghanaians from Nigeria uncovered hundreds of thousands of illegal migrants. Some half a million Colombians may be living clandestinely in Venezuela. About 25 percent of the population of the Ivory Coast are foreigners, many having migrated from Upper Volta and other Sahelian countries.

What happens when the economic bubble bursts and there is no longer any employment for foreign workers, when there is not even enough work for the native-born citizens of the country? Nigeria has provided one answer with its sudden mass expulsion of Ghanaians. The arbitrary and cyclical nature of economic differences between countries is pointed up by Ghana's expulsion in 1969 of all aliens without residential permits, forcing some 200,000 persons, mostly Nigerians, to leave. The recent massacres of Bangladeshis residing in Assam, a state of India, is still another example of what may happen when a large immigrant population competes with natives for insufficient land or jobs. Such solutions may well be repeated again and again in other parts of the world.

In the United States there is increasing concern with immigration issues involving refugees and both legal and illegal immigrants. Since the mid-1970s we have accepted well over 100,000 refugees every year, and given the unstable political situation in many regions of the world, one can only speculate as to the demands in future years. Since 1980, legal immigrants to the United States have averaged more than 600,000 per year. To that we must add the untold hundreds of thousands of clandestine immigrants who enter the country without legal documents. Their number is simply not known. Some illegal immigrants return home each year so that estimates of net illegal migration range from as low as 100,000 to upward of 500,000 per year. In particular, the number of clandestine entrants across the 2,000-mile border between the United States and Mexico is increasing as economic and political conditions deteriorate in parts of Latin America.

The situation in Western Europe is somewhat different. In Switzerland, Sweden, West Germany, and France, the 1960s and early 1970s saw a growing need for unskilled workers from other countries. Between 1960 and 1974 every major country in Western Europe had a positive net migration of legal "guest workers." France accepted 3.8 million workers; West Germany, 6 million. The early movements tended to come from countries such as Spain and Italy, but by the late 1960s and early 1970s the sources of immigration had changed dramatically. Poorer countries such as Morocco, Tunisia, Turkey, Yugoslavia, and Portugal had become the main sources of workers for France. In West Germany, over the same period, the Yugoslav and the Turkish proportion of immigrants increased so that by the early 1970s, Turks accounted for 39 percent of net immigration. Many of these workers came without their families. After 1973, economic conditions worsened in Germany and elsewhere and the demand for labor lessened. Under these economic conditions, some nations attempted to repatriate "temporary" workers to their home countries. Those efforts usually took the form of financial incentives often made only on the condition of permanent exile. Such repatriation programs have not been very successful. Guest workers have become permanent legal residents, and European governments have allowed some family reunifications. Nevertheless, the question remains: What does a country do with the foreign workers already there, particularly in a depressed economic situation?

Another very touchy issue has arisen in the more developed nations. Fertility has fallen to historical lows in almost every one of these countries. Women in West Germany are averaging 1.4 births; in Sweden 1.6; in Great Britain 1.7—all well below the level needed to replace the population. Without immigration the populations in these countries will soon begin to decline. Such a decline has already begun in West Germany, Denmark, and Sweden, and a number of other Western European countries are expected to begin losing population by the year 2000. With immigration, or at least with the higher fertility of the immigrants already there, the total populations may not decline, but within fifty to seventy-five years what were once homogeneous nations will hardly be recognizable. The Turks and Yugoslavs in Germany and Sweden, the Portuguese and North Africans in France, the West Indians in England, will all become significant minorities in these countries. This could result in new kinds of assimilation. More likely, however, rivalries between groups will become more intense and bitter, possibly leading to major disturbances.

In the United States, fertility has remained well below the population replacement level for more than a decade. Without continued immigration the population would begin falling after the year 2020. If the current pattern of migration were to continue for a century, the former, so-called white non-Hispanic majority would make up less than 50 percent of the population. This country is a "nation of immigrants," and at the turn of the twentieth century it experienced major ethnic changes in its white population as the main source of immigration shifted from northwest Europe to southern and eastern Europe. As we approach the twenty-first century the nation is faced with a new challenge: accepting millions of newcomers, this time of predominantly Asian and Hispanic backgrounds. Whether orderly assimilation will take place or increased racial conflicts will occur remains to be seen. One thing is certain: in the emerging era of high international migration, the concept of the nation-state and its cultural identity will be called into question. Emerging trends are forcing upon us some difficult ethical questions for which there are no real historical precedents.

Does an independent nation have the right to block immigration or to expel recent and not-so-recent immigrants if their presence is perceived as jeopardizing the economic well-being of the native inhabitants? The overly inhumane and violent measures taken in Nigeria and Assam are merely drastic examples of more extensive problems.

We have noted the repatriation attempts made by Western European nations. In the United States more than one million apprehensions of those engaged in illegal entry occur every year. These people are sent back to their home countries, but many return again and again. The U.S. Congress is currently wrestling with the issue of amnesty. Should the millions of residents who have lived and worked here for years without documentation be granted the legal right to remain or should they be repatriated?

Many in the United States feel that numerical increase should come to an end and be followed by an era of zero population growth at perhaps 275 or 300 million. Even with our very low fertility the population will, if immigration continues at recent rates, approach 350 million within a hundred years and will still be growing. Furthermore, the existing culture of the nation will be altered by the increasing proportion of immigrants and their descendants in the population. Thus ethical considerations are raised that go far beyond the matter of competition for jobs. Does a nation have a right to determine its own demographic and cultural characters?

The problems are not limited to countries with a long history of receiving immigrants. Tiny Belize, with a population of fewer than 150,000 people and independent of Great Britain only since September 1981, is faced with massive refugee and immigrant movements from El Salvador, Guatemala, and Nicaragua. Predominantly black and English speaking, Belize could easily become Hispanic through immigration. Barbados, population 250,000 with fertility below replacement, is concerned about current immigration from neighboring, poorer islands; some Barbadians are worried that their nation's culture will be changed by the incursion of East Indians. Such agonizing issues face many nations. Is it proper for a nation to insist that its culture remain as it is? If the answer is yes, is this a subtle new form of racism or is it a laudable expression of cultural identity?

The Universal Declaration of Human Rights adopted by the United Nations General Assembly in 1948 states unequivocally: "Everyone has the right to leave any country including his own and to return to that country." This "right" is hardly honored by many countries—witness the tragic plight of Jews trying to leave the Soviet Union. But even if all the members of the United Nations were to uphold the right of emigration, of what value would it be if no concomitant right of immigration had been agreed to? As a U.N. document reports, "There are few countries which have not placed restriction on the number of immigrants who may enter or upon the activities of the immigrants after arrival."

While there are no easy answers, I believe that action on a variety of fronts might help to reduce the future political and social stresses that will be caused by international migration. For one thing, massive economic as well as family-planning assistance must be supplied to developing nations if both population growth and emigration are to be curtailed. Assistance that contributes to labor-intensive rather than capital-intensive industry and agriculture should be emphasized. As countries like the United States and Japan become increasingly technologically oriented, more assembly-line work should become available in developing countries. To the extent that residents of these nations are able to share in global economic growth without leaving their homes, migration pressures will be reduced.

I believe that the developed countries must be prepared to accept changes in the age and ethnic composition of their populations. Even with increased economic and family-planning assistance to developing nations, any substantial reduction in the level of migration cannot be assumed for the near future. As a result, those of us in the developed countries must prepare for major changes in the composition of our future populations. We will be older societies simply because of our low fertility rates, and we will be more heterogeneous because of continued migration. Sweden may not be as Swedish in fifty years as it is today; West Germany may not be as German. The United States may be on its way to becoming a truly multiracial society, with no single population group constituting a majority. Such changes will occur, but they should not be allowed to come about so abruptly as to make a nation unrecognizable in a mere half century or even a century. Immigration must be limited to some reasonable level; nevertheless, it is important that the receiving nations consider innovative approaches to the acculturation of their newest residents.

The American people, while accepting continued immigration, must decide if they prefer a multicultural, integrated society, with perhaps two or more working languages, or whether every effort should be made to assimilate the newest immigrants into what many have traditionally considered the American culture to be—an Anglo-Saxon umbrella covering a limited variety of customs. Similarly, the heretofore homogeneous societies of Europe must decide whether they will assimilate their newest residents or maintain ethnic enclaves, where the residents, while integrated in some respects, will remain Turkish or Moroccan or whatever, and not become German or French.

Finally, the very size of international population movements of all kinds begs for a reexamination at the global political level of the issues involved. No nation has an open-door policy today. Yet migration is bound to increase in the future into precisely those nations that now exercise restriction on how many and what kinds of people are to be permitted to enter. A thorough discussion of alternative solutions to the new challenges posed by migration must be on the agenda of future international meetings, beginning with the United Nations World Population Conference, to be held in 1984 in Mexico City. The international community must seek some agreed norms of conduct in a world that combines increased disparities with increased mobility. Conflict and suffering are inevitable, but we must do what we can to hold them to a minimum.

# BIBLIOGRAPHY

An asterisk (*) preceding a reference indicates that the article or part of it has been reprinted in this book.

## BOOKS AND PAMPHLETS

Adler, Stephen. International migration and dependence. Gower. '80.

Baca, J. S. Immigrants in our own land. Louisiana State University Press. '79.

Bryce-Laporte, Roy. Sourcebook on new immigration. Vol. 18. Ayer. '79. Vol. 19. Transaction Books. '80.

Cafferty, P. and Chiswick, B., eds. The dilemma of American immigration: beyond the golden door. Transaction Books. '83.

Cordasco, F. and Alloway, D. N. American ethnic groups: the European heritage. Scarecrow. '81.

Crewdson, John. The tarnished door. Times Books. '83.

Cummings, Scott. Immigrant minorities and the urban working class. Irvington. '83.

Danilov, Dan. Immigrating to the U.S.: who is allowed, what is required, how to do it. I. S. C. Press. '80.

Davie, Maurice. World immigration. (The World Economy Series) Garland. '82.

Graham, O. L. Jr. Illegal immigration and the new reform movement. Federation for American Immigration Reform, 2028 P Street NW, Washington, D.C. 20036. '80.

Hofstettr, R. R., ed. United States immigration policy. (Duke Press Policy Studies) Duke Press. Forthcoming.

Jones, Catherine. Immigration and social policy in Britain. Methuen. '80.

Kramer, Jane. Unsettling Europe. Random House. '80.

Kritz, Mary, ed. U.S. immigration and refugee policy. Lexington. '82.

Lewis, S. G. Slave trade today: American exploitation of illegal aliens. Beacon. '80.

Lous, A. B. An immigrant speaks. Vantage. '81.

Maidens, Melinda, ed. Immigration: new Americans, old questions. (Editorials on File Series) Facts on File. '74.

Marshall, F. R. Illegal immigration: the problem, the solution. Federation for American Immigration Reform, 2028 P Street NW, Washington, D.C. 20036. '82.

Miller, M. J. Foreign workers in western Europe: an emerging political force. Praeger. '81.

Miller, R. M. and Marzik, T. D., eds. Immigrants and religion in urban America. Temple University Press. '77.

Nann, Richard C. Uprooting and surviving: adaptation and resettlement of migrant families. Kluwer Academic. '82.

Newland, Kathleen. Refugees: The new international politics of displacement. Worldwatch. '81.

Papademetriou, D. G. and Miller, Mark, eds. The unavoidable issue: U.S. immigration policy in the 1980s. Institute for the Study of Human Issues, University City Science Center, 3401 Market Street, Philadelphia, PA. '83.

Piore, M. J. Birds of passage: migrant labor and industrial societies. Cambridge University Press. '79.

Rodriguez, Richard. Hunger of memory. Godine. '81.

Sobel, Lester. Refugees: a world report. Facts on File. '79.

Tanton, J. H. Rethinking immigration policy. Federation for American Immigration Reform, 2028 P Street NW, Washington, D.C. 20036. '79.

United Nations. International immigration policies and programmes. (Population Studies Series, vol. 3) United Nations. '82.

Weintraub, Sidney and Ross, Stanley. Temporary alien workers in the United States: designing policy from fact and opinion. Westview. '82.

## PERIODICALS

America. 149:202. O. 15, '83. Refugee policy and politics.

*America. 146:206-9. Mr. 20, '82. The uneasy immigration debate. John W. Donohue.

*America. 150:208-9. Mr. 24, '84. The refugee problem: a look at the numbers. F. Moan.

America. 150:449. Je. 16, '84. Debating immigration reform.

*Atlantic. 252:45+. N. '83. Immigration: how it's affecting us. James Fallows.

Black Enterprise. 13:20. S. '82. A shaky freedom. M. York.

*Black Enterprise. 13:51+. Mr. '83. From other shores. Udayan Gupta.

Business Week. p 112. My. 30, '83. Control illegal immigration.

*Business Week. p 126+. My. 14, '84. Illegal immigrants: the U.S. may gain more than it loses.

Challenge. 24:44+. Ja./F. '82. Demographic links to social security. Peter Morrison.

Christian Century. 100:650-2. Jl. 6-13, '83. The undocumented alien and the law. H. Cortez.

Christian Science Monitor. p 22. F. 6, '84. Europe's besieged immigrants. Kevin Michel Capé.

Commonweal. 110:389-90. Jl. 15, '83. Half-open door: the puzzle of immigration. Jeremiah Baruch.

Commonweal. 111:295-6. My. 18, '84. Seeking sanctuary: a special duty for the U.S.? Mark Gibney.

*Congressional Digest. 62:195-224. Ag./S. '83. Proposed immigration reform and control legislation.

Current History. 82:429-32. D. '83. Migration and unemployment in Mexico. Marvin Alisky.

Department of State Bulletin. 82:63-5. F. '82. Population growth, refugees, and immigration. R. E. Benedick.

Department of State Bulletin. 83:56-7. Ag. '83. Soviet Jewry. Elliott Abrams.

Department of State Bulletin. 83:66-71. Ag. '83. Refugees: a continuing concern. James Purcell, Jr.

*Department of State Bulletin. 83:59-65. D. '83. Proposed refugee admissions for FY 1984. E. J. Derwinski.

Esquire. 99:47+. My. '83. The latinization of America. T. B. Morgan.

Esquire. 100:607+. D. '83. The emigré. Elizabeth Hardwick.

Foreign Affairs. 60:358+. Winter '81. Coping with illegal immigrants. Sylvia Ann Hewlett.

Futurist. 16:4-8. D. '82. Why the U.S. closed its borders. Richard Lamm.

*Humanist. 43:12+. Mr./Ap. '83. A new immigration ethic for the U.S.: updating the golden rule for the global village. Gerda Bikales.

*Humanist. 44:5+. My./Je. '84. U.S. immigration policy and the national interest. Georges Fauriol.

Los Angeles Times. sec 1. p 1. D. 14, '82. Economic impact: alien's role: it depends on who is being asked.

Los Angeles Times. sec 16. p 16+. O. 6, '83. Population, immigration, and the U.S. Richard Strout.

Los Angeles Times. p 1+. Ap. 1, '84. Millions drawn to El Norte by dream.

*Maclean's. 96:20-1. F. 14, '83. An exodus of the unwelcome. Val Ross.

Monthly Labor Review. 105:31–7. F. '82. Select commission suggests changes in immigration policy—a review essay. Philip Martin.

*Nation. 237:289+. O. 8, '83. Supply-side immigration reform. Geoffrey Rips.

National Catholic Reporter. 20:1–3. My. 18, '84. On trial in Texas: is it legal or not to help refugees?

National Catholic Reporter. 20:27–8. Je. 8, '84. Capitol hill run-around mars immigration debate.

Nation's Business. 71:4. D. '83. A time for statesmanship. J. J. Kilpatrick.

*Natural History. 92:6+. Ag. '83. Human waves: large-scale international migration. Leon Bouvier.

*Newsweek. 103:11. F. 27, '84. Don't close our borders. Julian Simon.

Newsweek. 103:18+. Je. 25, '84. Closing the door?

Newsweek. 104:24+. Jl. 2, '84. Immigration: reform at last. Tom Morganthau.

New York Times. p E 16. F. 13, '83. Time for a global code on migrations (letter). Jagdish Bhagwati.

New York Times. p A 2. Mr. 24, '83. A myriad of newcomers change face of Australia. Richard Bernstein.

New York Times. p A 14. My. 8, '84. The unpredictable fate of immigration reform. Robert Pear.

New York Times. p A 1+. Jl. 17, '84. Immigration bill questioned on the Texas-Mexico border. Robert Reinhold.

*New York Times Magazine. p 22+. My. 9, '82. The new Asian immigrants. Robert Lindsey.

New York Times Magazine. p 90+. My. 20, '84. From Poland, a new breed of emigré.

Nuestro. 7:19. Je./Jl. '83. U.S. must set a limit on refugees. Richard Salvatierra.

People. 18:101. D. 6, '82. To open the door or close it: an expert evaluates the explosive issues of immigration (interview with Lawrence Fuchs). J. Stickney.

Publishers Weekly. 225:35. My. 18, '84. U.S. writers speak for "forbidden writers."

Scientific American. 246:41+. Mr. '82. Illegal migration. Charles Keely.

Time. 121:18+. Je. 13, '83. The new Ellis Island. Kurt Andersen.

Time. 121:26–7. Je. 13, '83. Losing control of the borders. Maureen Dowd.

*Time. 123:40+. F. 6, '84. Rising racism on the continent. J. Nielsen.

*U.S. News & World Report. 94:37+. Mr. 7, '83. Invasion from Mexico: it just keeps growing. William Chaze.

U.S. News & World Report. 95:43. Jl. 4, '83. It's the immigrants who can move dramatically (interview with John Higham).

U.S. News & World Report. 95:50. Ag. 22, '83. Not all America's immigrants are huddled masses. D. Wiessler.

U.S. News & World Report. 96:62. Mr. 5, '84. Battle over curbs on illegal immigration.

U.S. News & World Report. 97:23+. Jl. 2, '84. Crackdown on illegal aliens—the impact. William Chaze.

Wall Street Journal. sec 2. p 29. My. 16, '83. U.S.-Mexican ties grow more tense.

Wall Street Journal. p 1. Ag. 11, '83. Popular haven. Gerald Seib.

Wall Street Journal. p 1. Je. 21, '84. Scores of U.S. churches take in illegal aliens fleeing Latin America. Geraldine Brooks.

Washington Post. p 87. O. 24, '82. Closing the doors to people in danger. Leo Cherne.

Washington Post. p A 13. Ap. 22, '83. Deciding which of the huddled masses may stay. Felicity Barringer.

Washington Post. p A 21. F. 22, '84. Myths about immigrants. J. J. Kilpatrick.

Washington Post. sec 2. p 7. F. 23, '84. Immigrant study topples another American myth. J. J. Kilpatrick.

World Development. 11:945–56. N. '83. Surplus labor as a source of foreign exchange. Martin Godfrey.

World Press Review. 30:32–33. S. '83. Southeast Asia's camps of misery. William Shawcross.